PLATES

Ceramic Arts Select Series

PLATTERS

Editor Sherman Hall

& BOWLS

PLATES

Ceramic Arts Select Series

PLATTERS

Editor Sherman Hall

& BOWLS

Published by
The American Ceramic Society
600 N. Cleveland Avenue, Suite 210
Westerville, Ohio 43082 USA

The American Ceramic Society
600 N. Cleveland Ave., Suite 210
Westerville, OH 43082

ISBN: 978-1-57498-380-7 (Paperback)

ISBN: 978-1-57498-589-4 (PDF)

Publisher: Charles Spahr, Executive Director, The American Ceramic Society.

Series Design and Graphic Production: Paula John, Boismier John Design

Assistant Editor: Forrest Sincoff Gard

Cover images: top: Bowl by Jared Zehmer; right: teapot by Jeffrey Nichols, bottom: mug by Lauren Karle.

Frontispiece: *Fruit of the Heart*, 7½ (19 cm) in height, press-molded vessel, altered and attached to wheel-thrown foot, carved exterior with glazed interior, by Antoinette Badenhorst. *Photo: Koos Badenhorst.*

Printed in China

TABLE OF CONTENTS

TABLE OF CONTENTS

FOOTED SLAB PLATES

by Liz Zlot Summerfield

Footed plate with underglaze, slip-trailed, and sgraffito decoration.

Handbuilt slab plates are a lovely addition to any potter's repertoire. They are versatile in use, and offer an open canvas to play with a variety of surface treatments. Although they only consist of two components, a slab and a foot, they are often loaded with pesky little problems. Here's a technique that is sure to provide you with a proud product.

The Issues

The weakest link in a slab plate is the foot. It's often uneven, off center, and unconvincing. A common technique is to add a coil, place the plate on a potter's wheel and throw it onto the slab. This often leaves a bump where the coils are joined and it has a tendency to crack. The fix to these issues is to create a foot ring and apply it as one cohesive piece.

Constructing the Plate

Starting out, consider keeping the plate shape simple: try a square, circle, or rectangle. Draw and cut out the shape of your plate on paper and make two copies of this shape. Save one to cut out the plate shape, and on the other draw a foot ring—this may take some experimenting as the size of the foot ring will alter the look and stance of the plate.

Cut out the foot ring by folding the paper in half, then cutting along your drawn lines. Once the paper foot is cut out, you'll be left with a stencil to help center the foot ring on the slab (see 1).

Roll out a slab large enough to trace around one plate template and one foot ring template. For smaller plates, I roll to a thickness of about

1. Create a pattern, stencil, and foot ring out of paper. Trace and cut the pattern and the stencil on a slab.

2. Attach the foot ring and refine its form to eliminate any unevenness and help connect the foot to the plate.

3. Gently press down in the center of the slab to shape the plate. Rotate the plate and gently lift all four sides.

4. Use a slip from your clay body to create a raised line with a slip trailer. Allow the lines to dry before applying underglaze.

⅜–½ inch. This thickness alleviates warping during the drying and firing processes. After rolling your slabs, it's important to run a rubber rib along the surface of both sides of the slab. This compresses the clay particles and removes any canvas texture from the working surface. Throughout the rest of the process, work on untextured surfaces such as drywall boards or a smooth fabric.

Trace the patterns with a needle tool before cutting them out with a knife. Hold the knife perpendicular to the slab and cut in one even motion (1).

Applying the Foot

Place the stencil onto the cut out slab and trace the interior ring with your needle tool. This traced line will act as a guide as to where to place the foot ring and keep it centered (see 1). Since both the clay slab and foot ring are the same consistency and very wet, you only need water to attach the foot ring to the slab. Brush water onto the slab and put the foot ring in place using the traced lines for guidance. Gently apply pressure with your thumb and index finger to affix the foot ring to the slab. Refine the finished foot ring to follow your aesthetic. Avoid using any additional water as you refine it and smooth just with your fingers. A rubber-tipped tool is useful in cleaning and blending the connection between the slab and the foot ring. The final step in applying the foot ring is to use a small roller to eliminate unevenness (2). Leave the plate upside down until it's ready to be flipped and formed.

Shaping the Plate

Success in handbuilding functional forms is about knowing the correct timing to touch the

5. Apply 1–2 coats of underglaze then gently scrape underglaze off the raised slip-trailed lines.

6. Carve subtractive lines into the plate using a sgraffito tool or sharp pointed tool.

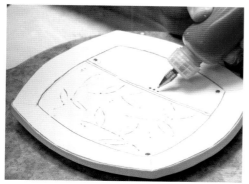

7. Add accent colors by applying underglaze using a slip trailer or brush.

The completed plate illustrating how the foot ring becomes an essential element of the whole design.

clay. When the plate reaches soft leather hard, flip it over onto its foot and place it onto a small board. Next, place the board on a banding wheel. Place your fingers under the plate and your thumbs on top of the plate and gently press down in the center (3)—you'll feel the foot ring under your thumbs. Press against the foot ring to create more depth in the plate. Use your fingers to gently lift the sides of the plate. Slowly work your way around the plate by spinning the banding wheel. Finally, look at the edges of the plate from eye level and make sure there is an even curve on all four sides. Gently cover the plate with plastic until it becomes stiff leather hard and appropriate for surface decoration.

Slip-Trailing and Carving Surfaces

When the plate reaches leather hard, it's at the appropriate stage to slip trail, carve, and apply underglaze, if desired. To create a raised surface, but not a change in color, use a slip with a yogurt-like consistency for slip trail application (4). Allow the lines to dry before brushing the entire plate with 1–2 coats of white underglaze. Once the underglaze is dry to the touch, take a metal rib and gently scrape it off the raised slip-trailed surface (5). This exposes the red clay and accentuates the slip-trailed drawing. To contrast the raised surface, carve accent lines using a sgraffito tool (6). Apply colored underglaze using a slip trailer or a brush for a small amount of accent color (7). Allow the plate to slowly become bone dry under thin plastic to eliminate warping.

Once the plate is bisque fired, damp sponge to clean the surface before applying glaze. For brushing, apply 1–2 coats of glaze the consistency of skim milk with a soft moppy brush and fire.

VOLUMINOUS
HANDBUILT PLATTER

by Ben Carter

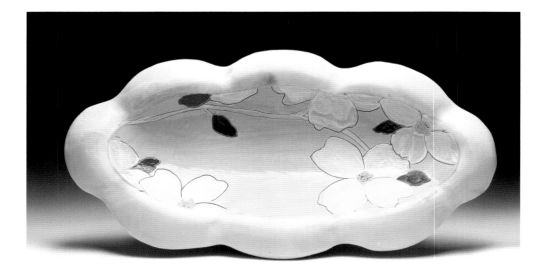

Dogwood Oval Platter, 20½ inches in length, created using templates and a slump mold technique, earthenware, painted slips, sgraffito, and glaze, fired to cone 3.

I begin a large platter by making a template in the shape and pattern of the rim of the platter, creating the template using tarpaper. Tarpaper can be used repeatedly because it's impervious to water. Cut the interior section of the template at both ends for easy registration on the form (1).

Next, create a slump mold from stacked layers of closed-cell foam (the kind used for home insulation). The thickness of the mold depends on the depth of the recessed area required in the finished piece. I'd suggest making the mold at least 3 inches thick for strength. Mark the outline of the template on the top of the stack. Individual sheets can be secured together us-

ing double sided tape. To create the recess in the slump mold, measure 1½ inches in toward the center from the two long ends and the two middle lobes of the outline and make a mark at each spot. Draw an oval connecting the dots, then use a serrated knife to cut out the shape.

Use the tarpaper template to aid in creating small cloth forms that sit on the rim of the foam mold. The cloth forms are comprised of eight semi-circular sections that form a wavy rim for the platter. Make each cloth form using two pieces of canvas sewn together and filled with heavy grog. Pin the thinnest edge or point of the cloth form to the foam using T-pins (2).

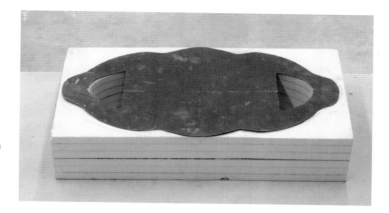

1. Create a tarpaper template of the platter. Make a stacked foam slump mold. Cut an opening in the foam 1½ inches in from the template's edge.

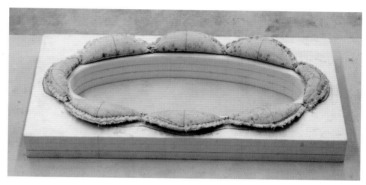

2. Use the tarpaper template to create a cloth mold that sits on the rim of the foam mold. Pin the cloth mold to the foam stack using T-pins.

Making a Platter

Cut a ³⁄₁₆-inch thick slab using the tarpaper template. Bevel or soften the edges of the slab and use a soft rubber rib to compress each side of the slab in both directions. Place the slab onto the stacked cloth and foam forms so that the slab edge lines up with the outside edges of the cloth form. Work the slab into the form using a soft rib and working both from end to end and side to side (3). The advantage of this form is the ability to bend the slab on more than one axis, so take time to work the clay down into the curves.

Let the slab firm up to a leather-hard. Place a bundle of soft padding and the section of blue foam that was removed earlier into the platter's interior. Flip the whole stack over (4). Make sure the rim rests parallel to your work surface and is elevated a few inches above it.

Make a ring to form the foot. Curve the wall of the foot into a slight "C" shape with the curve flaring away from the center of the piece. Try to match the volume of the foot to the volume of the rim. Allow the foot to set up to the same leather-hard consistency as the piece before attaching it by slipping and scoring (5). After the foot has set up and can hold up the rest of the platter without slumping, flip it over and remove the padding and foam. Smooth out any marks made by the foam.

Allow the piece to dry slowly under a loosely wrapped layer of thin plastic. Dry larger pieces, like platters, for about a week before bisque firing. Since pieces longer than twelve inches in any direction have a greater chance of cracking during the bisque fire, lightly sprinkle the kiln shelf with fine sand and place the piece on top of the sand.

3. Roll out a slab and trim it to the size of the tarpaper template. Place it so that the clay edge lines up with the edges of the cloth. Rib the slab into the mold.

4. Sandwich the removed oval section of blue foam, the cloth, and the platter (still in the slump mold) between your hands, then flip the piece.

5. Be sure the rim sits parallel to and several inches above the table. Add a foot to the bottom of the piece and allow it to firm up.

THROWN HANDLED PLATTERS

by Mike Guassardo

A handled platter is ideal for fruit and salads, and for serving. Provided you are using the proper clay body, you can also use it as a baking dish, as long as it is preheated along with the oven and not taken over 390°F (200°C).

Platters look deceptively simple to make, as creating one involves very basic throwing, but the larger scale translates into specific technical and design challenges. The form needs to be well constructed so that it survives the drying and firing processes, as well as years of use later on.

Because the platter form is so large, it will be a focal point on the table. In order to integrate all of the parts, the character of the pot needs to be addressed early on, and followed through in the finishing details. Handles can serve both a functional and visual purpose on very large platters. Of course, they make it easier to carry,

but they also provide an area where you can exercise your design sense. As shown here, thrown handles echo the construction of the platter, and can visually continue a line started in the rim.

Throwing the Platter

To get started, you'll need 10 pounds of clay and an 18-inch bat, a fettling knife, rubber rib, metal trimming tool, needle tool, a sponge and chamois, a kitchen scouring pad and a Surform tool.

Center and open up the ball of clay, leaving about ½ inch-thick base in the center (1). If you are not used to throwing large pieces of clay, make sure that the clay you're using is a little softer than normal, and slow the wheel down slightly as you center. Use both hands if necessary to create the center opening: overlap your

1. Center and open the clay, leaving a ½ inch thick base.

2. Slow the wheel down and pull out the clay to create a base that is 17 inches in diameter.

3. Smooth and compress the base using a rubber rib.

4. Create the rim in the thickened upper wall section.

hands, and use the upper hand to reinforce the pressure of the fingers that are in contact with the clay as you create the center hole. This steadies your hands and help with the added resistance of a large piece of clay.

Slow the wheel down slightly. Pull (or push) out the clay so that the base of the platter is about 17 inches in diameter (2). Using the palm of your hand, smooth the clay out evenly. This will condense and strengthen the base at the same time. Use a rubber kidney to finish compressing the bottom, smooth out the throwing lines and giving a slight rounding of the base as it meets the wall (3).

Starting where the base meets the wall, thin and pull up the wall about halfway. Take care not to thin this bottom wall section too much, or it won't be able to support the thickened rim. By stopping halfway, you've given your-

self a lot of clay at the top to create a distinctive rim shape.

With your fingers supporting the outside of the rim, press down with your thumbs on the top of the clay to define the rim (4). Keep your thumbs tightly together. Repeat this until you are happy with your rim, then go back and pull up the half-thrown wall to its full height. When you're finished throwing, the walls should be about ¼ inch, and the piece should be about 3 inches high.

Always check your base thickness when you finish throwing. It should be at least a quarter of an inch at the side and a little thicker in the center. Your cutting wire will tend to lift slightly at the center and the slightly thicker bottom allows for this. About an hour after throwing, trim off excess clay from the outside edge of the base with a pointed wooden knife tool and use a fettling knife to undercut the pot about a ½ inch

5. Create an undercut using a fettling knife.

6. Throw an open bottom cylinder for the handles.

7. Create ridges that match the rim pattern.

8. Trim the leather hard platter using a Surform rasp.

in from the edge to help facilitate your cutting wire (5). Since the pot is still attached to the bat, and therefore centered, the indented ring made by the knife on the bottom of the pot is accurate to the center of the pot while the clay edges are often not. This ring will also help you center your pot for trimming.

Cut the platter from the bat about an hour after throwing, keeping the wire pressed down on the bat as you run it under the base. After running the wire under the piece once, rotate the bat ¼ turn and run the wire under again.

Throwing the Handles
After you've finished throwing the platter, set it aside to dry and create the handles. The handles designed for this platter come from a thrown ring and attach to the top of the rim. Center a 1-pound ball of clay and open it all the way

through to the bat. Pull the open doughnut of clay out to a diameter that leaves enough clay to form an upright ring about 1½ inches high (the width of your pot rim) (6). Supporting the inner wall and the rim with one hand, use two fingers to push into the outside wall to form a shape with similar ridges as your pot rim (7). Cut into the outside of the circle with a fettling knife and repeat on the inside taking care not to cut all the way through which could distort the thin walls.

Assembling the Pot
When the platter is leather hard, center it upside down on the wheel and use a Surform tool to flatten and trim the bottom and sides of the platter (8). Use a steel kidney to smooth the bottom and sides. Finally, cut a 45° bevel on the edge. This gives a precise mark for where

9. Cut handle shapes, and clay balls for reinforcement.

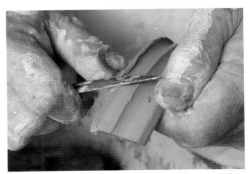

10. Trim excess clay from the bottom of the handle.

11. Attach clay balls to the handles and the rim.

12. Smooth the handle and rim with a chamois.

to start cleaning the underside after glazing and, on the completed piece, creates a shadow that gives the platter a slight visual lift.

When it's leather hard, cut a suitable length for each handle from the thrown ring, slicing it vertically down to the bat. Then, make eight balls of clay, each a little larger than a marble, for reinforcing the attachment between the handle and the rim (9).

Use a sharp knife to trim the sides of the handle that were attached to the bat (10). This will roughly resemble the thrown top. Using a damp scouring pad (Scotchbrite), roughly smooth the cut edges. Finish off with a sponge.

Divide the platter in half visually and make a small mark on opposite sides of the rim. Take the crescent shaped handles, dampen the edges and gently work them backwards to form flattened out areas to attach to the platter. On each side of your marked edge, score the rim and apply slip. Place the handle in position over the slip and push down and along the joint attaching the handle to the platter. Dip one ball of clay in water or slip (I add a little vinegar to these because it helps clay adhesion) and place it at the base of the handle. Supporting the underside of the rim, press down and along, attaching the ball to the handle and rim (11). Repeat the process with the remaining balls of clay, using four for each handle. In addition to reinforcing the join, the added clay provides a visual transition between the handle and rim. Clean up the handles and rim using a wet chamois or piece of leather (12).

FULL-TEXTURE PLATTER

by Annie Chrietzberg

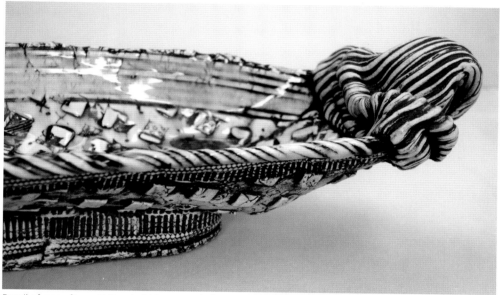

Detail of one of Lana Wilson's richly textured platters.

Lana Wilson's career spans more than 40 years and includes a vast repertoire of form and surface considerations, which she regularly shares with students.

Lana worked with functional stoneware for the first seventeen years of her life in ceramics. And then a job at a community college caught her eye, so, at age 43, she went back to school to get her master's degree. For Lana, graduate school completely changed the course of her work. "Number one, it opened up the way to lots of exploring and experimenting, which has never ended," she said. "Number two, I started making non-functional work and using the electric kiln exclusively, neither of which I'd ever done before." Now, Lana's focus has returned to functional pieces. She told me one reason: "I want my grandchildren to eat off of things that I made."

Texture Throughout

Lana applies texture in layers, and does so throughout her making process. During my visit, she made a serving platter to demonstrate how she works.

After using a slab roller to make a large slab, she lays out some fruit netting on the table, and sets the slab on top of it. This netting forms the basis of the texture composition on the back of the piece, though Lana will embellish it more at later stages. After smoothing the front of the slab with a small squeegee, Lana uses a wooden rolling pin from a pastry store to lay down some waffle texture, which cre-

1. Smooth out a slab, layer, and press in objects then texture the surface.

2. Use hand tools, stamps, and found objects to embellish the slab.

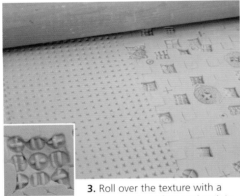

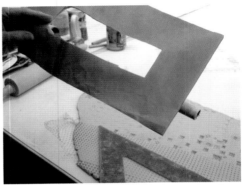

3. Roll over the texture with a rolling pin, to soften and tuck in the marks (detail shown in inset).

4. Use a handmade, paper viewfinder to select the best part of the textured surface.

ated impressed squares, then in an adjacent area, she lay down and rolled over plastic sink mats that left larger, high-relief squares (1). I watched her then target and go after some of the high relief squares with her small hand-held stamps, and some found objects, inverting them with embellishment (2).

I was surprised when she picked up her rolling pin and rolled over the work she had just done (3), but she explained to me, "You see, this softens it and makes it more interesting. I don't want it to look like plastic surgery. I don't like the whole Southern California glitzy sequin scene, I like old, worn friends. I like layers; I walk regularly in the Torrey Pines State Reserve when I'm home in San Diego. I love those layers of information around me."

I looked, and the effect she had created by rolling over existing texture was to "tuck in" all the little marks she had made, like treasures in lockets. After tucking in her preliminary and secondary texture with a rolling pin, Lana embellished further with one of her new favorite items, the red scrubby applicator from a Shout bottle, and an old favorite, a seamstress' marking tool.

Forming the Platter

Lana had created a slab much larger than what she actually needed for the piece she had in mind. She cut a framing device out of a piece

5. Cut out a dart then use it as a pattern to cut the remaining darts.

6. Lift and connect the edges where the darts have been removed.

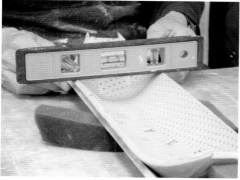

7. Prop the piece up, level the sides with a spirit level, and adjust as needed.

8. For handles, shape cones from large triangles cut from a textured slab.

of paper roughly the proportions of her intended serving dish (4). She used this view-finder to locate the best part of her texture drawing, marked the boundaries cut out the shape by using a straightedge.

Lana needed to take two darts out of each end to have the flat shape rise up into the form she wanted. She took the triangular piece of clay she removed, turned it over, and set it gently down to trace it where she wanted the second dart. She then took those two cut-outs and placed them on the other end, and traced and cut out the remaining two darts (5). The size of the dart determines the shape of the final form. After slipping and scoring, she simply lifted and butted the joining edges together (6), and then

used small pieces of foam to prop up the ends of the serving dish which allows them to firm up while supported. She fills in gaps in the texture where the darts were removed with paper clay to prevent cracks from forming along the seam.

To address the sides, Lana grabbed a couple of paint stirring sticks, which she used to lift the sides and then shoved pieces of foam beneath to hold them in place. She filled in gaps that had been made by cutting through existing texture on the edges, and then compressed and beveled those edges with a pony roller. Then, she used a spirit level to make sure the edges, were, um, level (7). "I don't know a gallery who would take a piece that's not level," she murmured as she made slight adjustments. "There we go!"

9. Lift and drop the cone two or three times to get an organic shape.

10. Slip and score the handle in place, then support it with foam.

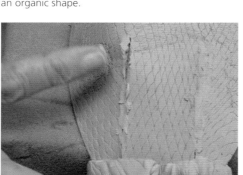

11. Turn piece over on foam supports, fill seams and adorn the repair.

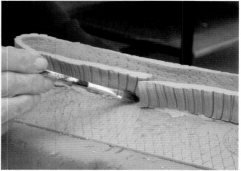

12. Make a foot from a long, thin piece cut from a textured slab.

Making Handles

The next task was to make the handles. First, she textures a slab and cuts out large triangles, then she rolls them into a cone (8), seals them using a pony roller, and drops them on her workbench (9). They magically gain character with each *whump*. Once she is satisfied with the result, she cuts away excess clay with a fettling knife, scores and slips the end of the serving dish, as well as the inside of a handle, and then attaches it, stacking foam beneath it for support (10).

Lana constantly manipulates the surface of her pieces as she is making, adding texture as she goes. After attaching the handles, she grabbed a wooden dowel with sharpened ends (a pencil would work, too) to both re-draw and enhance existing lines. After the piece had

dried to leather hard, she removed the bolsters and turned it over on a large piece of foam to access the bottom. She filled the gaps in the seams with paper clay, again to strengthen them and prevent cracking (11). When she makes a repair like this, she adorns it. "I could teach a whole course on cheating," she joked, while rolling a seamstress' marking tool over the filled-in seam.

Adding a Foot

The last part of the serving dish project was to make and attach a foot. Before she had turned the piece over, she had taken an approximate measurement with a seamstress' measuring tape, and had created a long slab to texture. She played around a bit with some scrap clay to determine the appropriate height, textured

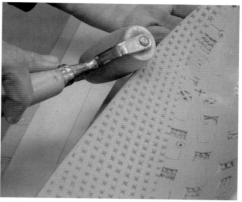

13. Smooth the foot with a roller and cut decorative arches through it.

14. Use a pony roller to bevel and finish both sides of the platter's edge.

the slab, and used a straightedge to cut a long strip of clay for the foot. She picked up the long strip in loose folds and dropped it a few times on the table. "This makes an undulating line I just love," she told me as she worked.

She placed the foot on the bottom of the pot, shaped it how she wanted it, and cut the excess away, then joined the foot into a ring. After scoring and slipping the areas that need joined, she attached the foot ring to the bottom of the serving dish and used a dry soft brush to remove excess slip and blend the seam (12). She then used a common loop tool to create a little looped arch on each side of the foot (13). She rolled the edge with a pony roller (14), used a ware board to flip the piece right side up, and used the spirit level again to make adjustments.

Lana has a delightfully free, direct, and easy way of making, but don't let that fool you into thinking she doesn't take her time in the studio seriously. "I've changed my style of work about six times through out my career, and each time it takes me about six months to a year to figure it out," she told me. "People don't realize that being an artist is really about daily discipline; when I'm working, I want my time to work. I'm not one of those ladies who does lunch. Ceramics is far too expansive for that."

Finishing

Lana Wilson's work is mostly black and white with bits of vibrant color splashed about. She says, "I have a background in painting, and this technique really appeals to the painter in me." She gleaned this current surface treatment from two artists, Denise Smith of Ann Arbor, Michigan, and Claudia Reese, a potter from Texas.

Simple Slip

To prepare the slip, Lana takes 100 grams of small pieces of bone dry clay and adds 10–50 grams of a stain. The percentages of stains varies according to the intensity of color she is trying to achieve.

The clay Lana uses is Half & Half from Laguna, formulated for firing at cone 5, though she fires it to cone 6. This clay body is half porcelain and half white stoneware. It's not as white as porcelain, but it does fire white rather than yellow in oxidation, isn't as finicky as porcelain, and works well with Lana's making methods. If you're buying clay from the East Coast, she suggests a clay body called Little Loafers from Highwater Clays.

Easy Application

The technique is simple. On a piece of bisqueware, first brush on black slip or one of the base

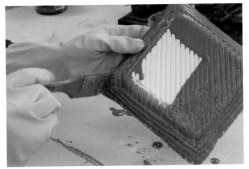

15. First brush on black slip or one of the other dark base colors below.

16. Sponge it off, leaving slip in the crevices.

17. Using colored slips, dab on bits of color here and there, particularly in the deeper texture.

18. Remove some of the colored slip with steel wool in order to bring the clay surface through again.

colors (15) then sponge it off, leaving slip in the crevices (16). Then, using colored slips dab on bits of color here and there (17). Remove some of that with steel wool (18). "I can't use water for this step or it will muddy the colors," Lana explains. After the piece has dried, Lana uses a clear glaze to seal the surface.

Recipes

There are two groups of colored slips. The first group Lana uses for the base coat that she washes off, leaving color in all the recesses. The accent slips are more intense and removed with steel wool. All stains are Mason stains except for 27496 Persimmon Red, which is from Cerdec. Add the stains and bone dry clay to water and allow to sit for 30–60 minutes so it will mix easier.

BASE COAT OR WASH COLORS

6600 Best Black	10%
6339 Royal Blue	5–10%
6069 Dark Coral	35%

ACCENT SLIPS

6129 Golden Ambrosia	30%
6485 Titanium Yellow	20%
6024 Orange	30%
6236 Chartreuse	50%
6027 Tangerine	15%
6211 Pea Green	50%
6288 Turquoise	50%
6242 Bermuda	10%
6069 Dark Coral	35%
6122 Cedar	25%
6304 Violet	60%
K5997 Cherry Red*	30%
27496 Persimmon Red (Cerdec)*	30%

* Inclusion pigments

LARGE PATTERNED PLATTERS

by Christina Bryer

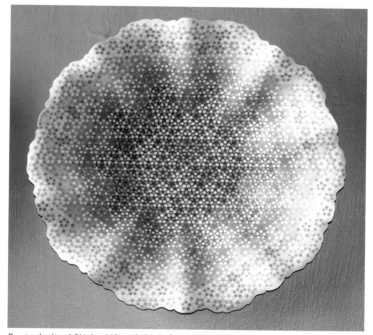

Pentaplexity, 16½ in. (42 cm), high-fired porcelain.

I have always been interested in geometry, and responded strongly to Roger Penrose's aperiodic patterns when I first saw them 15 years ago. In his writing/research, I encountered pentaplexity and realized, "this is it." In these grids, the patterns of pentagons do not tile regularly, but aperiodically (1). The geometry in my art is inspired by this aperiodic tiling pattern and Euclidian lace. In short, the patterns reflect the geometry of life and nature's tendency to construct complex geometries on micro and macro levels such as DNA strands and stellar configurations. Starting with absolute grids frees one to work with infinite possibilities.

Constructing a plate takes an entire, uninterrupted working day. I begin by preparing my tools: three or four plastic bottles with different size nozzles, a jug of porcelain slip, a fine silk cloth, a firm cotton cloth, a graphic print, a brush, a wooden skewer, and ten pre-made and high-fired porcelain cones (2). I start in the morning by preparing a basic porcelain slip (see recipe on page 20). For this plate I only use white porcelain slip, but one can add oxides or stains for different colors.

I soak a plaster bat in water to keep the humidity constant for a day (3). A dry bat is not a desirable surface to work on as the drying clay slip starts to flake off. I then dampen the graph-

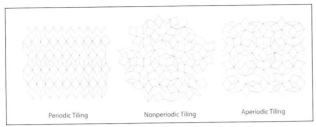

Periodic Tiling　　　Nonperiodic Tiling　　　Aperiodic Tiling

1. Examples of periodic, non-periodic, and aperiodic tiling patterns.

2. Materials: Four plastic bottles with different sized nozzles, a jug of porcelain slip, fine silk cloth, firm cotton cloth, a graphic print, a brush, a wooden skewer, and a flat plaster bat.

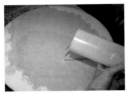

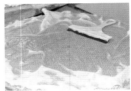

3. Soak the plaster bat in water to keep the humidity constant for a full day.

4. Detail of the enlarged aperiodic tiling print used as a drawing guide. Place it on the bat.

5. Dampen the print and place it face up on the bat. Smooth out a layer of water-soaked fine silk on the print.

6. Make dots with different sized nozzles. Start in the middle and work toward the outer edges.

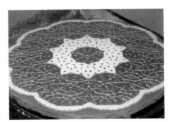

7. The creative process begins when dots are selected and connected to lines in spontaneous patterns.

8. Once you feel the pattern is complete, spray it at an angle with a darker terra sigillata to coat and enhance the pattern.

9. The next step is to systematically cover the whole back with porcelain slip. Cover the entire pattern, one section at a time.

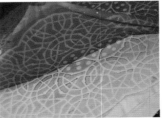

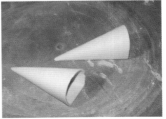

10. After the entire pattern is filled in, let it rest until it is no longer tacky. Then cover the plate with a layer of silk then a layer of firm cotton.

11. Place a sturdy piece of plywood on top and gently flip all the layers over at once. Slowly peel the silk away from the porcelain.

12. Make sure the reusable, premade, slip-cast, porcelain cones are clean and dry. Have several on-hand for various patterns.

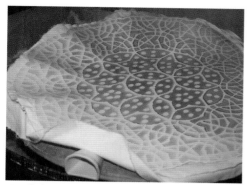

13. Lift the patterned porcelain slab by gently pulling the bottom cotton cloth upward then push the cones underneath to create an undulating pattern.

14. Let the plate completely dry then carefully remove the cones and tug gently on the silk until the porcelain is completely free.

15. With open hands for maximum support under the porcelain, gently lift the plate onto a kiln shelf. Dust the cones with alumina to prevent them from sticking then re-insert them and fire.

16. Fire the plate to 2300°F (1260°C). The finished piece can vary slightly in thickness and size. The finsihed piece is less than a ½ inch thick and is about 17 inches (42 cm) in diameter and quite translucent.

ic print (4) which is a master grid of 20 inches (52 cm) in diameter (I print to this size because it is the maximum size I can fit into my kiln and it can just be lifted onto a kiln shelf when it is dry without disintegrating in my hands), constructed in Adobe Illustrator and printed on archival paper. It can be re-used many times and has the added advantage of non-directional stretch (normal paper, when wet, stretches much more in one direction than the other, which will skew the pattern). I then smooth down a layer of fine, water-soaked silk on top of the print with a squeegee (5). The clay slip will stick to the paper and the layer of silk between

the paper and the clay facilitates the peeling off of the paper later.

Next, I use different sized nozzles (a brush or a stick will also work) on the plastic bottles to start making dots with the porcelain slip (6). I start in the middle and work toward the outer edges. As far as the final plate is concerned, I work from the front toward the back, which means that the marks I lay down first will be top most in the final product.

The creative process begins when I select dots and connect the lines in between them (7). No two plates will ever be the same as there is no prescribed sequence or plan. I let the pattern in the grid take me where it wants to go; in other words infinite variations or interpretations are possible—every decision and every mark I make affects the final outcome.

I work on the pattern from one position, turning the wheel to work on new sections. I find that working on a potter's wheel or a banding wheel makes it easier to avoid smearing the marks I have already laid down.

After completing the whole pattern for the plate, I spray it at an angle with terra sigillata to enhance and bring out the pattern (8). I then cover the whole back with a thicker porcelain slip layer that forms the basis of the plate (9, 10). I fill in each section individually rather than pouring one single layer, this way the slip follows the pattern, making the back reflect the front. Trial and error have taught me that 2.2 pounds (1 kg) of mixed slip is sufficient to cover my 20-inch (52 cm) plaster bat.

I let the plate rest for at least three hours until it is no longer tacky. I then cover the plate with a layer of silk plus a layer of firm cotton to facilitate ease of handling. The cloths prevent the bat from sticking to the clay, the silk leaves hardly any imprint on the clay, and the cotton cloth adds strength. I now cover it with a light plywood bat, flip it over, and peel the silk up and away from the porcelain (11). The result is a porcelain pancake resting on top of two layers of cloth. (I re-use the cotton, silk, and paper over and over again.)

The reusable, slip-cast, high-fired porcelain cones now come into play (12). I lift up the decorated porcelain slab by gently pulling the bottom cotton cloth upward and pushing ten porcelain cones underneath to create alternating humps and slumps (13).

The plate is now left to dry completely, which can take up to several days depending on the weather (14). Once it is dry, I carefully remove the cones and tug gently on the silk until the

porcelain is completely free. The silk tends to stick very slightly to the dry porcelain but comes away with gentle tugging. For maximum support, I place my open hands under the porcelain and gently lift the plate onto a kiln shelf. I re-insert the cones under the plate for the firing (15). Each cone is dusted with alumina to prevent it from sticking to the plate during the firing. I fire the plate to 2300°F (1260°C). The finished thickness can vary slightly but my pieces are generally less than ½-inch (1–2 mm) thick and about 17 inches (42 cm) in diameter and quite translucent (16).

Reusable Supports

To make a mold for these cones, I slab build a cone to the desired slope and size. When it is leather hard, I refine and finish it, then make a plaster cast. I dry the plaster mold for several days and then cast porcelain slip into it. I usually make ten cones from the same mold and fire them to cone 9 (see 12).

BASIC PORCELAIN SLIP
Cone 9

Potassium Feldspar	25 %
Kaolin	60 %
Silica	15 %
	100 %

Add: Water . . . . up to 400 g
Deflocculant. . . . . .5 ml
Methyl Cellulose . . . . 1 tbsp

Mix 2.2 lbs. (1 kg) of slip for a plate 20 in. (52 cm) in diameter

I use Alcasperce for my deflocculant. Other types may require different amounts. Methyl cellulose (the main ingredient in wallpaper pastes) can be used as a mild glue to give extra green strength to delicate pieces.

SLIP INLAID PLATES

by Robert Strasser

Slip-decorated plates and platters, stoneware and earthenware, clear glaze. (Shino glaze on top and bottom left plates), various firing temperatures, 2012–13.

When I was in college and just a few years into making ceramics, I took a two week trip in early summer to England. My primary goal was to meet as many potters as I could. The experience deepened my love of English ceramics and introduced me to a technique that has been one of the most exciting veins in my studio work ever since: wet slip surface inlay.

I had read briefly in Bernard Leach's *A Potter's Book* about slip application and how to get surface marbling and feathering patterns on flatware using slip trailers to decorate thin slabs of clay. There in England, in the studio of his son David Leach, I got to see in person my first finished examples of feathered slipware. On the same trip, I visited the Victoria and Albert Museum and had the opportunity to see a large, and particularly fine, marbled dish with an amber lead glaze made in Staffordshire in the early 1700's. I wanted to reproduce these effects, and

1. Roll out a slab of clay onto a piece of canvas, place it on a ware board, and apply a layer of white slip over the whole surface. While the base layer of slip is still wet, create a pattern of concentric circles and dots using a contrasting slip.

so my creative journey making slip-ware began.

I started by experimenting with methods of slip preparation and application. It was exciting and more fluid than any method I had ever tried. I was quickly hooked. In addition to feathering and marbling, new patterns that I hadn't seen elsewhere appeared in my work. Echoes of natural patterns such as wood grain, minerals, and the skin and fur of animals emerged in the liquid slip I was applying to slabs of clay. Even microscopic biological patterns were suggested by some patterns. It was truly mesmerizing, with each round of new work segueing into the next. As I translated my love of the natural beauty found in the world around me into my work, I was also thinking about how human creative endeavors recapitulate nature.

I begin the process with two or more slips of equal viscosity, ho-

2. While the slip is still fluid, tilt the board supporting the slab to distort the pattern. Varying the angle, direction, and amount of time the slip is allowed to flow all affect the final result.

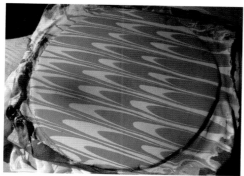

3. Once you have a pattern that you like, allow the slip to dry out so that it is not tacky to the touch. When the slab reaches soft leather hard, it is ready for forming.

4. Lay a hump mold on top of the patterned slab, positioning it over the area that you like best. Having a slab that is larger in diameter than the final size needed is helpful here.

5. Place a board on top of the hump mold, and grasp it and the board supporting the slab, and sandwiching the mold and slab together firmly, flip the stack over remove the board, then peel away the canvas.

6. Press the slab around the hump mold gently using your fingers. Smooth over the canvas texture lightly with a metal or rubber rib at this point.

mogenized through 40-mesh screens. A base white slip can be colored with stains to develop as large a palette as desired. A darker slip provides contrast, making patterns bolder. It is very important to screen the slips immediately prior to use or they tend to settle and flocculate, causing the edges to bleed during and/or flow irregularly after application. Rubber slip applicators are filled with the various colored slips to be used in decoration (conserve resources by starting simple with just two slips, expanding the color palette once sufficient comfort with the process minimizes material loss).

Cut or roll out clay slabs and put them on cloth scraps for handling. I form slip-decorated slabs over hump molds, so I make them about an inch larger than the edges of the hump molds to be used for making dishes. Place a slab on a ware board and begin by flooding the wet slab with slip, tilting the board to spread it out evenly over the entire surface. The inlay colors can be applied onto this base slip with a steady hand in whatever pattern and combination is desired (1). Straight lines work well for feathering and marbling, while dots in alternating colors create concentric cells that, when tilted, flow into elongated shapes (2). These circles can be manipulated into a pattern that resemble wood grain when stretched by tilting the ware board in opposite directions.

Once an appealing pattern is achieved, set the slab aside for about a day to allow it to

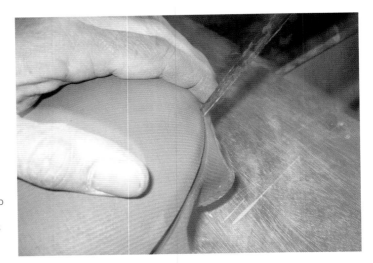

7. Using a fettling knife, remove any excess from the slab that hangs below the hump mold. Creating an even line is easiest when using the edge of the mold as a guide.

8. Feathered oval slip dish, 9 in. (22 cm) in length, stoneware with very thin shino glaze, fired to cone 10 in reduction, 2012.

dry until it is no longer wet to the touch, yet still flexible (soft leather hard) (3). When the slip surface can be touched lightly without smearing, it's ready. A bisque or plaster hump mold is centered over the slab (4), the two are inverted, and the cloth peeled off (5). Push the slab down gently, wrapping it around the profile of the mold (6). Trim the excess slab with a knife along the mold's edge (7), smooth the rim gently with a fingertip, and flip it over onto another board. Remove the mold carefully, pulling it straight upward. As the piece dries, the rim can be cleaned up with a fettling knife. It should be rotated daily to avoid warping.

The primary consideration for glazing is to avoid treatments that will mask the slip decoration. I typically use transparent or translucent glazes that show off the patterns underneath, but a very thin application of opaque glaze such as the shino applied to this piece gives the surface additional depth (8).

MARBLED PLATTERS

by Michelle Erickson and Robert Hunter

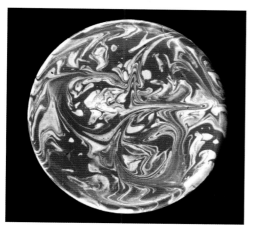

Left: Marbled dish, Italian slipware, ca. 1620–1640 (from the Chipstone Foundation collection).
Right: Dish, Staffordshire or Midlands, 1720–1750; slipware, 13¾ inches in diameter (Image courtesy of the Colonial Williamsburg Foundation).

For thousands of years, potters in many cultures have used slip or liquid clay to create decoration. The technique was elevated to an industrial level in seventeenth-century Staffordshire, England where potters produced a wide variety of dishes and hollow wares for the international market. American archaeologists unearth English slipware fragments in prodigious quantities from seventeenth and eighteenth century historical sites. Contemporary art potters have also found inspiration in these traditional English slipwares, popularized by the work of Bernard Leach and his students.

The creation of marbleized patterning where two or more colored slips are laid down and manipulated to produce a variegated appearance is among the most common slipware decorating techniques. The English technique of marbling may have had its origins in the early seventeenth-century marbled slipwares of Northern Italy (above left). Early American slipware potters working in many parts of the colonies also employed marbleizing methods in decorating their wares (above right).

How It Works

Gravity and centrifugal force are key elements for inducing the movement or flow of the slips during the marbleizing process. The term "joggling" is used to describe the physical act of controlling this movement which requires very specific, and somewhat awkward looking, body and arm movements. The degree of aesthetic success is directly linked to the skill of the potter in controlling the flow of the slips. It is interesting to note the words of Bernard Leach who suggested turning slip-trailing mistakes into marbled decoration: "When one or more slips have been *unsuccessfully* [emphasis added] trailed over a wet background . . . it is sometimes a good plan to try for a marbled effect by violently shaking and twisting the board upon which the clay rests." Leach's assertion implies that the mixing of two or more colors of slip to produce marbled patterns seems a fairly random and haphazard process but the opposite is true. It actually requires a thorough mastery of the materials and physical control of the slips.

Understanding the nature of slip is important as its properties can vary from one extreme to the other. When using slip, the clay particles tend to fall out of suspension fairly quickly so that the potter needs to frequently stir the solution as it has a very short working life. As soon as slip comes into contact with a drier surface, it begins to stiffen immediately. It is analogous to working with molten glass. Unlike glass though, slip can not be "reheated" or remoistened. A mistake made in applying a slip means living with it or wiping it off and starting over.

Tools, Techniques and Materials

The essential tool needed for slip trailing and marbleizing was (and still is) the slip cup. The trailer itself was a small, clay vessel although leather, fabric or animal horn may have also been used. The concept of the trailer was simple. A small tube, reed or quill was inserted into the trailer, which would be filled through a top hole. The potter could regulate the flow of the slip by covering the top hole that also served as a vent. In order to flow freely, the viscosity of the slip had to be maintained through frequently shaking, and adding water or a thicker slip mixture throughout the process

In most instances, slip is poured or dropped onto another surface. Rarely is it brushed on; the clay surface is usually damp, which causes the slip to be streaky or uneven. Although brushing can produce very accurate lines, it also necessitates

building up several layers to achieve a smooth surface. Pouring slip, however, instantly creates an even, opaque covering, making the best use of the materials and the potter's time.

The clays used for making the slips must have similar shrinkage and drying rates. The slips then have to be prepared with similar viscosity. Poorly prepared slips can produce an unsatisfactory flow and impede the marbling process.

The Process

The making of a Staffordshire style marbled slipware dish begins with a flat clay disk or slab rolled out to a consistent thickness. The slab is supported on a board or bat to bear the wet and still plastic clay.

Pour a coating layer of slip over the slab, covering the entire exposed surface, allowing the excess slip to drain off (1).

Immediately thereafter, trail a systematic series of lines in a contrasting slip across the entire surface (2). Hold the tip of the slip tube above the surface as it should not touch the wet base slip. The distance between the tip of the slip tube and the surface of the ground slip dictates the width of the lines; the further from the surface, the wider the line.

 Evidence from original examples like the Staffordshire or Midlands Dish suggest that the lines were laid down in very specific, proscribed patterns which runs contrary to the suspicion that the marbling process used a more random application of slips. The edge of the original example is the key to determining the original configuration of the white slip lines. There is more white at the edges and patterns loop back from this point all around the piece, which indicates the series of lines was trailed on, one at a time, in a continuum within the confines of the slab disc, doubling back for each consecutive line (3). This observation was critical to deciphering the trailing process employed by the 18th century Staffordshire potters to achieve this specific marbling technique.

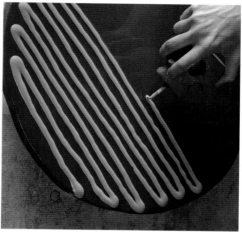

1. Place a rolled-out slab of even thickness on a circular wooden bat. Flatten out and trim any overhanging clay. Holding the board, pour a black ground slip over the slab.

2. Immediately afterwards, trail parallel lines of white slip onto the wet ground. The consistency and moisture content of the slips must allow both to flow easily without running.

3. The prepared slab immediately before joggling. Note how the white slip lines doubled back at the edge of the slab. This is key to achieving a pattern similar to the original dish.

4. The beginning of the marbleizing process. The slab, resting on the bat, has been rotated or "joggled" to start the flow of the slips.

After the slip lines are systematically applied, the clay slab, still supported by the bat, is then tipped and rotated using gravity to coax the slips to flow (4). This process will create a pattern of swirls (5). If the slip is too watery, the lines will run and blur. If the slip dries too quickly, the slips will not flow properly. Two conscious aesthetic and practical decisions have to be made:

How much time can be expended before the wet slips stop flowing; how to judge when to stop before the lines of color lose their separation and become muddy. Because both slips tend to firm up quickly, the elapsed time for joggling is usually thirty to forty-five seconds.

The now marbled slab is set aside to allow the slips to dry further (6). Before the vessel

5. The marbleized slab in the process of joggling. Supporting the bat while rotating it to move the slip. Both slips will firm up quickly, the elapsed time for joggling is usually 30–45 seconds.

6. The marbleizing process complete. The decoration is still on a flat slab. Before forming the vessel, the slips must be allowed to set up to prevent marring of the marbleized surface.

7. After sufficient drying (when the surface is no longer tacky to the touch) the slab is draped over a hump mold and pressed into place to form the dish.

8. Finished and glazed marbleized slipware dish by Michelle Erickson, 13¾ inches in diameter, 2001 (from the collection of Judge Henry D. and Mrs. Kashouty).

is formed, the slips must be allowed to set up to prevent marring of the marbleized surface yet the slab and the newly slipped surface must remain pliable. If the slab becomes too dry, it will crack. If the slips are still too wet, the slab will stick to the surface of the mold. After the slips are no longer tacky or wet to the touch, the entire slab, which is still plas-

tic, is removed from the bat and placed over a "hump" mold surface down and pressed into shape (7). These molds were typically made of fired clay although a plaster one is being shown here. Allow the dish to dry further to a leather hard stage. The irregular edge is trimmed with a knife to form a completely circular form and the rim is then crimped or pressed with a coggle wheel to create a pattern. The molding process helps flatten the slips and after glazing, the surface is smooth (8).

Further Exploration

In the case of most English flatware, the marbled or combed decoration is created before the form. Marbleizing on hollow forms takes place, however, after the vessel has been created, usually by throwing. The ground slip is either poured over the vessel or it is dipped into a container of slip. Contrasting colored slip is then trailed on, again in a systematic fashion. The vessel is then tilted and rotated to control the gravitational flow of the slip creating a variegation of the wet slips.

In addition to marbleized patterns, the same technique, without the joggling, can be used to create distinct images using contrasting slip. Slip is poured onto the surface then a design, image or pattern is trailed onto the wet surface. The slipware chargers above are examples of this technique.

Materials

As a ceramic artist my methodology is integral to my study of early ceramic techniques and the process of experimental archeology, using objects and fragments from ceramic history to rediscover the mysteries of the processes and materials used to create these wares. Obviously in the 21st century there are numerous commercially available materials to create a spectrum of palettes and glaze surfaces. For my purposes, however, I have chosen to develop all my own slips and glazes often using indigenous clays, metallic oxides, carbonates and sulfates and basic raw ceramic materials to create all of my glaze formulas as needed.

Suggested Clay and Slip

For cone 04 red earthenware, I use Standard's 103 (grogless) and 104 (with grog) clays and Laguna white earthenware (Miller 10) for slip decorated creamware and pearlware, which I also fire to cone 04. For slipware, a starting point would be to use your clay body (no grog) for a base. This way, you will be starting with slip compatible to your clay and glaze formulas. You can often buy dry bags of the clays you use and add various commercial stains to achieve the palette you want. I use metallic oxides, which tend to be more problematic but can offer rich results. Also, if you are looking to make a dark slip, start with an iron rich clay; it will require less colorant. Just try to find one compatible with the white or light clay/slip in terms of the firing range and shrinkage.

Tip

Do not use deflocculated slip (casting slips) for slip trailing and marbling, as the viscosity is counterproductive to this process.

Suggested Glazes

The piece I illustrated is a dark brown/black slip ground with a white slip trailed on top and the gold color of the finished piece comes from the addition of iron to the low temperature clear glaze. There are many commercially available clear glazes and you can add a commercial yellow stain for the effect. I use iron oxide to give my own cone 04 formula its yellow gold hue to closely resemble the lead glazed Staffordshire slipwares. As I do not use lead on functional wares, I often use more temperamental ingredients that have small firing ranges and require a lot of experience in glazing and firing, so I am not including those formulas as they are not user friendly nor safe.

It is important to test fire new slips and glazes. I find my small test kiln invaluable and I will often take it up slowly and down fire it to more closely resemble the conditions in the large kiln. All my pieces are fired in electric kilns but they do not self-fire and I do not use kiln sitters as my glazes are finicky and require manual manipulation of temperature.

BIG PLATTERS THE EASY WAY

by Yoko Sekino-Bové

Throwing large pieces (generally more than 10 pounds, or 4 kg) is an exciting challenge for any potter; however, many people of smaller stature hesitate to muscle out big pieces. It feels like an emotional, as well as a physical, challenge. I felt the same way until learning how to produce large serving platters in an effective way at a tableware studio where I worked as an apprentice. Following their instructions, and some techniques from my own experience, I found that throwing large flatware, such as plates, platters, and shallow bowls, demands less physical strength and promises a higher success rate compared to making tall shapes because you don't have to lift a high wall of clay on the wheel.

TOOLS

- 2 large smooth bats
- A smooth shower curtain cut to the shape and size of your bat
- Sponge
- Ribs
- 2–3-inch-thick stiff foam
- Wooden paddle (optional)

4 Tips to Success

To reduce the physical work and hassle, there are four things you can do when getting ready to throw a large platter.

1. Make sure that the clay you're using is soft. You don't need the clay to be firmer like you

would for throwing a tall form, and it's less of a burden on your wrists while expanding the clay if it's soft. When using a fresh bag of commercially-prepared clay that's too big to wedge, slam the bag on the floor a dozen times from different angles to condition the clay.

2. When you place the clay on the wheel, lay it on its side in relation to the spiral created from wedging (1). You will want to make the clay into more of a circular mound, but the illustration shows the orientation of the spiral.

3. The larger the plate, the greater the chance of an S-crack appearing. Allow freshly wedged clay to rest for at least a few weeks before using it to create big platters.

4. Check the inside diameter of your kiln. You can throw a plate or platter up to the exact size of the kiln and, as it dries, it shrinks enough to fit.

Throwing Process

To make the wide platter shown here, I used 25 pounds of clay and a 24-inch-diameter bat. Place the bat on the wheel head then wet the surface. Place a circle cut out from a shower curtain on top of the wheel head. Make sure the curtain fits tightly and there are no trapped air bubbles (2). The shower curtain layer removes the need for using a wire tool to separate the platter from the bat, allowing the clay to release more easily when it's flipped over and ready to trim.

Place the clay on the bat and start beating it down to a mound shape while slowly turning the wheel. Use dry hands (3) or a wooden paddle (4) and apply even pressure.

Flatten the mound to create a cake shape about 3 inches high. If you want to have a high rim for a bowl shape, keep the mound about 4–5 inches high. The diameter of the cake shape will be the size of the foot ring of the piece (5).

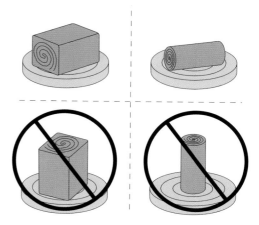

1. Place the clay on the wheel so that the spiral pattern from wedging or pugging the clay is not facing up.

Using a wet sponge and wet hands, open the form. Leave about 1 inch of clay between your fingers and the bat. Once the center hole is created, pull out toward you while also pressing down lightly with both hands to create a flat bottom (6). While you expand and compress the bottom, move your hands from the center to the rim, then from the rim to the center several times. This throwing back motion can redistribute the clay and make it even (7). It takes several passes to fully open up the form. Finally, use a rib to smooth and compress the flat surface.

Once the bottom is open and compressed, start forming the wall. Pull up, compress the top, then move your fingers back down the vertical wall, compressing and essentially "pulling down" to keep it even. Keep the wall straight (8). Leave enough clay on the rim, which will support the structure by tension.

Using a very wet sponge, slowly open the rim (9). When you flare the wall out, start from the rim and move your hands down the wall toward the center to keep the desired angle and prevent collapsing. When deciding on the final angle, factor in that the rim will move upward

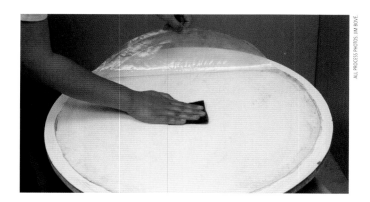

2. Dampen a large bat and smooth the cutout shower curtain on top of the bat.

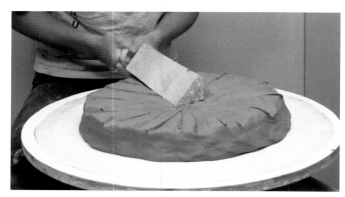

3. Place the ball of clay onto the bat and pound it into a mound with your hands while the wheel spins.

4. As the wheel spins, use a wooden paddle to further compress and flatten the mound.

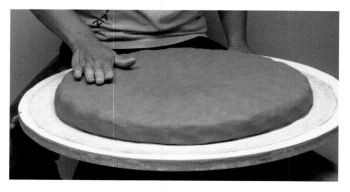

5. Finish the process by pounding the clay with your hands again until you get to the diameter you want.

6. Wet your hands and hold a wet sponge in your dominant hand. Press down with both hands to open.

7. Flatten the bottom moving your hands from the center to the edge and back again.

8. Pull up the wall using the index finger on the inside and a sponge and knuckles on the outside.

9. Using a very wet sponge, slowly open the rim. As you angle the wall out, work from the rim down.

as it dries. The opening angle will be 10° to 20° steeper when dry.

Once the form is thrown, leave it uncovered for a day or two, depending on the humidity. In drier regions it may be necessary to cover the rim with a ring of plastic to keep it from drying too quickly.

Trimming

To trim the platter, you'll need to flip it over. If it's a low, wide form, trying to lift it off of the bat directly and flip it would cause extreme distortion, so sandwiching the piece between two bats works better. To avoid ruining the platter, you may need another person to help

flip the big platter onto the second bat to prepare for trimming.

Place a foam sheet on the center of the platter to support the wide bottom while flipping it over. The foam should be taller than your platter rim in order to press against it firmly enough to support it. Cover it with a second bat that's larger than the diameter of the platter (10).

Use a flat surface to help with flipping. Create a pivot point by having one edge of the bat remain in contact with the table. Hold the bats together tightly to prevent slipping, lift one side up and flip the bat sandwich over as quickly as possible, maintaining contact with the pivot point to help steady the process and

10. Place a foam sheet onto the center of the plate for support while flipping it over.

11. Rest one edge of the bat on your wheel head as a pivot point, hold the bats tightly, then flip them over.

12. Carefully, peel the shower curtain sheet off of the platter.

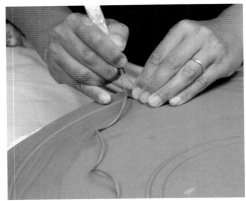

13. Trim the outside of the foot ring, mark the interior support ring, then trim between the two rings.

take off some of the weight (11). This works better than trying to flip it in the air. Peel the shower curtain sheet off (12).

Center the platter on the bat. Its own weight keeps it secured to the bat, so you don't need to place clay coils around the edge.

Trim the outside of the foot ring first to define the platter's silhouette. The foot ring itself should be almost as wide as the rim, to allow for support. A center ring prevents potential sagging of the center part, so define that area, then trim away the excess clay between the two rings. The amount you trim away depends on the thickness of the bottom of your platter. For this platter, which started with a bottom

thickness of 1 inch, I trim away about ⅔ of an inch of clay inside of each foot ring, leaving a bottom thickness of just over ⅓ of an inch. Make sure the inner ring(s) are not taller than the outer ring by checking with a straight edge (13 and 14).

For hanging, carve a deep groove into the outside of the foot ring (15). This is less stressful to the foot ring than puncturing holes. After firing, use a loop of picture hanging wire placed in this groove to hang it.

Flip the platter right-side-up using two bats and the sandwich method again and check the weight and appearance of the foot ring. Before the platter reaches the bone-dry stage, flip the

14. Use a ruler or a level to check that the second foot ring is not taller than the outer ring.

15. If you plan to hang the plate on the wall, carve a deep groove into the outside of the foot ring.

16. Flip the plate back onto a clean, dry bat, and always transport it carefully to avoid warping and cracking.

platter occasionally to let it dry out evenly and to prevent warpage. Always move the platter by picking it up with the bat while it dries. Don't pick up the platter by the rim; it may cause warpage or cracks (16).

Firing Tips

- Always place a big platter in the center of the kiln for even heat distribution. The foot of the platter should be completely supported on a level, smooth shelf, otherwise cracking and warping can occur. Don't place the platter so the base spans two shelves. It may help to fire the platter on a thin layer of fine grog or on a waster slab made out of the same clay body to allow for lateral shrinkage during the firing. To prevent the rim from cooling off faster than the center part, which can lead to cracking as the rim contracts more quickly than the rest of the platter, evenly surround the rim with kiln posts. Alternately, when firing low, wide work, make sure there is adequate airspace between the rim of the platter and the shelf above it. Allowing air to flow freely helps to minimize the temperature difference between the middle of the shelf and the outer edge.

- Do not place other objects on the platter during a bisque firing. This can cause it to warp or crack.

- Most of the center cracks happen during the cooling process, not in the heating process. It will help big platters survive the thermal shock if you can slow down the kiln's cooling process, either by ensuring the kiln is fully loaded, or by including a down-firing ramp schedule in your firing program. The weight sometimes makes a big platter stick to the kiln shelf during the glaze firing. Make sure the kiln shelf is covered with kiln wash, and apply a thin layer of alumina hydrate solution to the unglazed foot ring.

LARGE PLATTERS WITH ALTERED RIMS

by Samuel L. Hoffman

(Top) Porcelain platter, 24 inches in diameter, wood fired in the Kent State University (Ohio) anagama, natural ash glaze and atmospheric flashing.

(Bottom) Stoneware plate, 12 inches in diameter, reduction fired in a gas kiln, carbon-trap shino glaze with wax resist brushwork.

Ceramic plates and platters are some of the most functionally useful forms you can make. They also provide wonderful surfaces for artistic expression and creativity. However, the process of creating a plate or platter does not merely entail squashing a piece of clay into a flat disc. In fact, when subjected to the high temperatures of glaze firing, a poorly crafted platter will inevitably crack, warp, or deform in some manner. Here is a technique for trimming that helps eliminate some

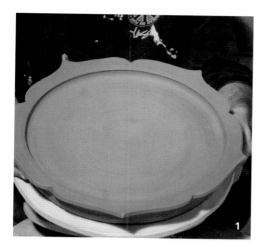

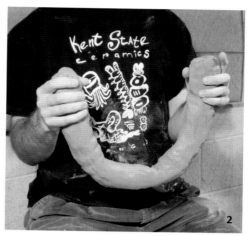

of the problems inherent to making large plates and platters.

Altering the circular form of a plate is an exciting means of expression for ceramic artists, but can present difficulties at the trimming stage (1).

If the rim of a plate is cut or manipulated into an asymmetrical shape, or is delicate, the piece cannot simply be inverted onto another bat for trimming (2). Instead, the piece must be placed on a clay chuck that supports the plate

in the center. To create this chuck, form a large coil from the same clay body that the plate was made from.

Attach the coil to the wheel head in the shape of a donut, making sure that enough height is established to hold the plate above the wheel head (3).

Flatten and smooth the coil using as little water as possible, creating a rounded cushion on which to rest the plate (4). It is important to let the plate stiffen up a little bit more than usual

before trimming to avoid flexing or chipping the altered lip when the piece is inverted.

Leaving the plate on the bat it was thrown on, carefully flip the plate onto the palm of one hand or a small bat the fits the center of the plate (5).

Place the upside-down plate onto the coil and make sure that it is centered (6). Gently press down on the middle of the plate to create a vacuum that will hold the piece in place (7). Start trimming by removing excess clay from the outside of the plate.

Trim the plate using the same techniques described before, taking care to avoid the delicate lip that hangs over the wheel head (8). When the foot rings are trimmed, smooth the bottom of the plate and carefully remove it from the coil. If the inside surface of the plate has been marred from resting on the coil, use a sponge to clean it up.

Although plates and platters are traditionally used horizontally for serving on a table, they can be prepared for hanging on the wall (9). One technique is to punch holes into the out-

er foot ring that can later be used for hanging with wire or string. Use one hole if you want to determine the orientation of the platter. Pierce several holes to allow the owner of the piece to determine the best way to hang it.

Another method of preparing a platter for hanging is to attach a simple coil of clay as a loop at the top of the piece, taking care that it does not protrude below the foot ring when the piece is sitting flat (10). This clay loop can be hung directly on a nail or can be used to attach a wire or string to the platter for mounting. It is possible to purchase prefabricated plate hangers, but most of these protrude over the edge of the piece, creating a visual distraction that takes away from the integrity of the rim.

Porcelain platter, 17 in. (43 cm) in diameter, reduction fired in a gas kiln, carbon-trap shino glaze with wax resist brushwork.

Porcelain platter, 22 in. (56 cm) in diameter, reduction fired in a gas kiln, carbon-trap shino glaze with wax resist brushwork.

SPLIT-RIM BOWL

by Emily Donahoe

Sarah Jaeger's simple, well designed serving bowl brings both food and cheer to the dinner table.

Geometric patterns and forms combine with organic, plant-inspired lines in artist Sarah Jaeger's inviting functional pots. In her hands, a modest, wheel-thrown serving bowl becomes something special with some easy alterations and a layered, wax-resist glazing technique.

The alterations developed over years of playing around with simple geometric forms—dividing up the space, making rounds into squares, and just seeing where things went.

"A lot of the evolution just comes from working on the wheel and doing something and then thinking, well, what would happen if I tried this?" she explains. "So it doesn't start out as high concept all the time."

Sarah says that the alterations are "both visual and tactile—and both of those things come into play with functional pots." Add to that Sarah's love of decoration and the surface of the bowl becomes a space where pattern and irregularity meet. She says her goal is to make a bowl that functions well, that's also beautiful and adds some joy and a sense of festivity to someone's meal. For her, it's about making things more joyful.

Throwing and Altering

Sarah's small but well-appointed backyard studio looks out onto a sunlit garden. Her dogs, Archie and Oona, laze nearby as she goes about her work.

3. Refine the split rim using a wooden knife or rib while supporting the rim on both sides as you work.

1. Define the split rim using the back of your thumb pressed down in the middle.

2. Use ribs on the inside and outside to compress the walls and remove throwing lines.

4. Divide the rim using a circle divider and marking tool. Press in at each mark, creating six lobes.

"This is, in many respects, a very simple pot," says Sarah as she centers a 4½-pound lump of clay on the wheel in preparation for making a serving bowl. She is working with porcelain, which she prefers because of its translucent quality. "With porcelain, even when the pot is unglazed or even if it is a monochrome glaze, you get a lot of interesting play of light and shadow that I think is very beautiful," she explains.

Throwing the bowl starts out normally, the clay is centered, opened to the desired depth and diameter. When making the initial center hole, Sarah purposefully leaves more clay in the floor of the pot. By not pressing down as

far when creating this hole, she leaves room for trimming a taller foot on the pot. Then, she starts to pull up the walls. To create the flange on the exterior of the bowl, she pulls up the wall of the pot halfway and then skips a vertical space of about an inch and a half, resuming the pull just above it. This leaves a thicker area that can be trimmed to shape later. She then splits the rim using the back of her thumb pressed lightly into the middle (1).

Next, she goes back to refine the shape of the bowl. As she works, she explains the process. "I did about two or three pulls with a sponge in my outside hand and then I go to using ribs (2). I use the curve of the rib to help me get the inside

5. Refining and smoothing the trimmed surface using a rubber rib to remove any lines or marks.

6. Draw a design on the inside of the freshly glazed pot using a pencil.

7. After painting in the leaf forms using a colored wash, trail on green glaze line decorations.

8. Additional red glaze decorations are trailed on next. The trailed glaze should be thicker so it does not run.

curve of the bowl; but also the ribs really help to compress the clay and make it stronger. After a few pulls with your hands, if you go and use the rib, it strengthens it, recompresses it. It also gets rid of all the throwing lines. Sometimes (the marks are) something you want to use visually and sometimes they're just distracting."

The split rim is further refined using a wooden knife (3). Using a sponge, Sarah cleans up the slurry from the inside of the bowl, then uses a thin piece of plastic to smooth out the rim.

The bowl is ready to be altered. Sarah drops a small circle divider into the bottom of the bowl as a guide and uses a chopstick to divide the rim

into six sections. Next, at each mark or divot, she presses the chopstick into the wall from the flange to the top, creating six lobes (4).

Trimming

When the bowl is leather-hard, Sarah centers and secures it for trimming. For heavier pieces, or pieces with very uneven rims, she uses a foam covered bat.

"I intentionally leave quite a depth of clay here, just because I want this pot to have a really nice, elevated foot. I want to be able to work with the proportions of the lip element and the volume element and then the foot, so

9. Use a tinted wax resist to visibly protect the painted and trailed patterns and shapes.

10. After the wax dries, paint a layer of wash, here copper sulfate, over the surface to create another layer.

a little extra clay leaves me some leeway to play with."

Using a trimming tool, Sarah removes excess clay from the bowl. As she trims, first creating the outer diameter of the foot and then the inside diameter, she taps the area she's working on every once in a while to gauge its thickness. She then trims another flange to echo the one she's thrown into the bowl. After she's achieved the shape she wants, Sarah removes excess clay until the bowl is of the right heft.

"I'm pretty fussy about the weight of the pots," says Sarah. "There's something about the way a pot looks that sets up an expectation for what it's going to weigh. With a bowl that I intend to be a functional pot, my goal is not to mess with people's expectations about what it is or how it functions."

After trimming, she goes over the surface with a rubber rib to smooth out any lines from the tool, and to refine the transition between the rounded bottom and the outer flange (5).

Decorating

Sarah works atop the New York Times Arts and Travel sections—after she's read the articles, of course. She wears latex gloves to protect her hands from the abrasive glaze. After

waxing the foot of the bisque-fired bowl with paraffin, she uses tongs to dip the bowl into a clear glaze, allowing it to dry for a bit before beginning the first step in decorating.

"This is another one of my secret tools: it's a no. 2 pencil," Sarah explains as she draws a simple leaf pattern inside the bowl (6), and then uses a paintbrush to fill in the patterns with a wash of rutile and Gerstley borate. She applies a thin layer for a translucent, cloudy effect (see 7).

As she works, Sarah explains that her decorations have evolved out of hand repetition and "responding to the curve of the pot."

"A lot of my glaze decorations started out as very geometric patterns and over the years evolved into more botanical patterns. The longer I did it . . . the more organic the lines and the forms and those decorative motifs became," says Sarah. "I like patterns that are pretty organized and symmetrical but then, when the pot gets fired everything softens and relaxes. There's a kind of nice contradiction there."

The next two glazes are applied in thick, dense lines. The first is Reeve Green, mixed very thick to give the bowl some texture (7). Sarah applies the glaze using Clairol color applicator bottles, which she gets at a beauty supply store. She then uses the same technique with an orange-red glaze, which is made from the same base glaze as Reeve Green, but with red inclusion stain added (8). On the outside of the bowl, Sarah uses the same elements in a different arrangement; she decorates the bowl all the way down to the underside of the foot, filling in the spots between leaves with simple waves and crosshatches.

"It's a three-dimensional pot," says Sarah. "I think it matters to pay attention to all of it." Plus," she adds, "when people wash dishes, they love that the undersides are decorated. One time this guy in California emailed me a photo of bowls in the dishwasher."

Wax and Wash

Wax resist is an old technique, but Sarah finds that she uses it a little bit differently than most potters.

"One thing that caused me to keep playing with this technique is that I really love surfaces that have a sense of depth," says Sarah. "It confuses that figure-ground relationship—and for some reason that confusion really interests me."

Sarah uses a color-tinted Aftosa wax to go over the decorations on the bowl with a Japanese-style brush (9). This type of wax helps her to see what she's done and also brushes on more easily than paraffin wax.

"The wax will repel anything that goes on over it. Some other waxes that flow and brush well don't seem to resist the cobalt sulfate as well as Aftosa," explains Sarah. "So I will paint with wax on all the parts of this that I want to remain what they are now."

Sarah's final step is to brush a cobalt sulfate wash over the entire bowl (10). She mixes the colorant with water by eye, testing it on newsprint to see that it is the right concentration before applying it. Sarah explains, "The form of cobalt sulfate that I use, because it's water-soluble, you get a really soft line. Just like when a watercolor goes on paper and it bleeds into the paper, as the water of the cobalt sulfate wash

REEVE BASE
Cone 10 (oxidation or reduction)

Custer Feldspar	75 %
Whiting	15
EPK Kaolin	5
Silica	5
	100 %

Add: Bentonite	2 %
Green: Chrome Oxide	4 %
Red: Cerdec Intensive Red	10 %

Used as the trailing overglaze colors. When trailing this glaze, it needs to be thick so that it does not run.

LIMESTONE CLEAR
Cone 10 (oxidation or reduction)

Custer Feldspar	27.0 %
Ball Clay (OM 4)	14.0
EPK Kaolin	7.0
Whiting	20.5
Silica	31.5
	100.0 %

This glaze is not an absolute clear. On its own in reduction, it's a little greenish.

evaporates, the cobalt bleeds into the glaze, so the line quality is really soft." **Note:** Cobalt sulfate, like all soluble salts is easily absorbed into the skin. It is important to wear latex gloves when working with this, or any other soluble salt colorant. It is not recommended to use this material in group studio situations.

As she finishes up the pot, Sarah reflects on the paradox of spending so much time discussing technique—and so much time decorating a single pot. "At the end, you don't want the person who is using the pot to think about technique at all. You don't want it to look like it was a lot of work; you just want it to look like itself."

LAID-OUT BOWL

by Jared Zehmer

Jared Zehmer used a dowel to achieve the final diameter, 11½ in. (29 cm), of the bowl without having it slump or collapse. After the bisque firing, he glazed the bowl with reduction and ash glazes, laid a piece of green bottle glass in the center to emphasize the throwing texture, then fired it to cone 10 reduction in a gas kiln.

This elegant form utilizes a brilliantly simple technique that I picked up during my years as a journeyman potter in Seagrove, North Carolina. The process uses a simple dowel or stick to lay out a bowl to seemingly impossible diameters without the worry or dread of it collapsing —as long as you stay within reasonable diameter, weight, and thickness ratios for the scale of the bowl you want to make.

The key here is not to wait to lay your wall out to the final width on your last pull. The wall of your bowl should be at or around a 45° angle by the time you have finished all your pulling and cleaning with a rib. Then it's easy to use a wooden dowel to lay it out the rest of the way.

The beauty of this technique is that you use the stick to push against the natural state and shape of the 45°-angled wall of the bowl. The clay's memory and its resistance to this laying out process prohibits the walls both from falling any further than you push them and from ultimately collapsing. So therein lies both the challenge and the fun; once you get comfortable with this technique you can push the limits with larger amounts of clay and even longer sticks to see how far you can lay it out.

The Preparation

About 2–3 pounds of clay would be an ideal starting point for this bowl, however for this

1. Open the bottom and leave a low-relief swirl in the middle.

2. Keep the walls and rim thick as you pull up.

3. Compress the walls using a wooden rib after the last pull.

4. Use the rib to do one last pull to widen the form, starting at the bottom of the piece and angling the rib.

5. Position the rib to angle the wall out to 45° as you move from the bottom to the rim.

demo I'm using 4 pounds. Center it pretty low and wide into the shape of a fat, 3×7-inch hockey puck.

Open the bottom to about 3 or 4 inches in diameter and leave an optional low-relief swirl in the middle. A later addition of a piece of green bottle glass placed on top of this swirl before the final firing makes a nice melted glass accent (1).

While keeping the walls and the rim thick, I usually do no more than four pulls to create the initial shape (2). It's better to leave them slightly too thick than too thin as you can always trim off the excess clay. If the walls are too thin, they won't support a low, wide, cantilevered bowl shape. After the last pull I clean and compress the walls using a wooden rib (3). Then I do another pull with the rib, this time angling the

wall to about 45° to prepare for the laying out (4 and 5). This is a cross section of the bowl at the point where I start laying out the bowl using the dowel. Notice the thickness of the walls (about ¼ inch) and the amount of clay left in the bottom foot area. This thick clay foot acts as extra support for the wall after the laying out process and can be trimmed away later (6).

Laying It Out

After cleaning the water out of the bottom I go back and saturate the sponge and give the inside and outside of the wall a good (but not too heavy) sheen of water; just enough to keep the stick and my hands from dragging. I'm using a ⅝-inch wooden dowel that's sanded on one end to a rounded tip so it won't leave any marks or

6. A cross-section of the thrown bowl shows the tapered thickness of the walls. The thicker bottom section supports the laid out wall.

7. Hold the dowel in your right hand, and support the outside wall with your left hand as you start to pivot the dowel down to widen to the bowl.

8. Slowly pivot the dowel, keeping the tip that's in the center of the bowl stationary, and moving the outer end down.

9. Stop pressing down on the dowel when the rim is two inches above the wheel head.

10. Trim a sharp-angled foot ring on the bottom to allow for attaching a hanging wire.

cuts inside the pot. Lightly placing the tip of the stick inside the bowl at the point where the wall begins, I hold the dowel in my right hand in an overhand grip while carefully situating my left hand underneath the wall for support (7). While you're getting accustomed to this process, it isn't always necessary to use your left hand for under-wall support, it's just something I've gotten used to doing. It's entirely possible to do the laying out with just one or both hands holding the stick steady as long as you press down very slow and carefully. Just pivot down with the stick while keeping the tip stationary (8).

Finishing

I tend to stop laying the bowl out once the rim reaches about two inches above the surface of the wheel head or bat (9). Because of the wall's thickness and lack of curvature, it's fortunately difficult to flop it from this point on. However,

if the bowl developed a split in the rim during the throwing process, it may weaken and form a tear in the wall, which is why you should attempt to keep the rim as thick as possible during throwing as it will naturally thin out during the laying out process. Something to keep in mind is that the walls will lift during drying, however that also provides an opportunity to put the bowl back on the wheel and push the walls further down. You will find this time around it's much easier and safer as the clay has stiffened.

Once the bowl is leather hard I like to trim a sharp-angled foot ring on the bottom (10). This angled foot allows for a medium-gauge, bendable wire to be wrapped around it for wall hanging, as these platters double as beautiful wall art. So there you have it. Be brave, and don't be afraid to try larger amounts of clay as this technique is very versatile.

UPSIDE-DOWN BOWL

by Martina Lantin

Clay naturally wants to move centrifugally so making large bowls can be challenging because it is difficult to keep the form on center. I make bowls from wheel-thrown parts assembled when leather hard. I throw the bases for the bowls upside down. By working the clay up and in from a centered ring, I'm able to form the base of a large bowl working from the rim to the foot without having to trim.

Unique asymmetrical bowls are made possible through this method of throwing and altering. When cutting the rim section from the wheel, hold the wire tight to the wheel head as you only pull it through one edge of the piece. Then allow the spin of the wheel head to cut the piece off completely. This helps prevent any distortion in the shape of bottomless forms.

Making the Parts

The bowl shown is made from three parts—base, bottom, and top. The base, a thrown slab, is added last; and the bottom is a basic bowl that's thrown upside down. The top is an open ring, and is the finished rim.

1. Make a bottomless ring, throw upward and inward to create a pleasing curve.

2. Use a flexible rib to smooth the interior and exterior to create a graceful arc.

3. Leave a bit of a foot on the rim section to help it stay attached to the wheel head during throwing.

4. Use a cheese slicer to refine and prepare the raw edge of the bottom for attaching the rim.

Begin throwing the bottom by making a bottomless centered ring. Throw upward and inward to create a pleasing curve (1). Define the rim, keeping in mind that it will serve as the foot. Rib both the interior and exterior to create a graceful arc (2). Cut this section from the wheel holding the wire tight to the wheel head.

Throw the top section right-side up from a centered ring. Explore a variety of rim profiles, being conscious of the edges and the shadows different shapes may promote. In this process it's especially important to remember to leave a bit of a "foot" on the rim section to help the wall stay attached to the bat while pulling up the clay (3). Wait to cut the rim from the bat until you're ready to attach it. Waiting helps keep the rim from warping.

Altering the Forms

Once the bottom has reached a firm leather-hard stage, turn it over and use a cheese

5. Cut the rim or top section into two pieces and score the bottom edge of each one.

6. Attach the sections to the bottom, then compress the clay on both sides.

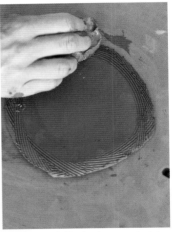

7. Measure the bottom aperture with calipers and shape the base slab accordingly.

8. Score and slip the base and add an additional supporting coil inside the foot ring.

slicer to refine and trim excess clay from the raw edge for attaching the top section (4). The asymmetry of the bowl begins to reveal itself at this stage. Remain conscious of creating a sense of fluidity and generosity as you work. Next, cut the rim or top section into two pieces (5) and attach using the traditional score and slip technique followed by compressing the clay on both sides with a rib (6). Attach the base last.

Measure the bottom opening with calipers and cut and shape the base slab accordingly (7). Score and slip the base (8) and add an additional coil inside the foot ring to reinforce the seam. Using a wet, pointed brush, clean and compress the join. While I strive for crisp visible seams and joins, these steps may also be applied to creating a seamless "upside down bowl" where the transitions blend together.

LARGE NESTING BOWLS

by Courtney Murphy

A few years ago, when I switched from cone 6 porcelain to low-fire earthenware, I was excited about the potential to work larger. I had come up with some ideas, and even made some sketches, but had never actually made anything very large.

I had been searching home improvement and salvage stores for years, looking mostly at lighting fixtures, but really any object with a relatively shallow continuous curve to make a mold from. Finally, a little over a year ago, I borrowed a giant mold shaped like a satellite dish from a friend. I was attracted to the gradual uninterrupted curve of this simple form, and the flexibility that it offered. It could be the basis for a large platter, a round-bottomed bowl or a rocking, boat-shaped vessel. Using his mold, I created both a hump mold and a slump mold out of plaster.

After making the plaster mold, I created a series of bisque molds off of the hump mold

to fit the larger bowls. I bisque all of my pieces nesting inside of one another inside the largest bisque mold. I also add a small amount of fine grog between each layer. The structure of the bisque mold prevents the rounded bottoms from warping or slumping in the kiln. Because I leave the pieces unglazed on the bottom, I can still fire my larger pieces inside of these molds for the glaze firings.

The larger pieces really benefit from having the extra support of the bisque mold, and firing them in the mold enables me to retain that continuous curve that I like so much. The smaller pieces in the set don't need to be fired in molds because they weigh less and have a shallower curve. They do well glaze fired in a pile of fine grog.

Having several bisque molds also allows for separating the pieces out to work on the inside of one, or to allow for more even drying with-

1. Cut bowl bottoms using templates. Smooth and compress the largest slab into the plaster slump mold.

2. Each slab bottom is added, separated by a thin cloth, then ribbed to conform to the curve of the one below it.

3. Cut slabs for the walls of the bowls, then taper and soften the rim edge with a rubber rib and sponge.

4. With smallest bowl in place, score the bottom edge of the wall and the edge of its base, Apply slip and join.

out the danger of the bottoms slumping or deforming in the greenware stage.

Now that I had this very large mold as a starting point, it was time to go ahead and try to create more significant pieces. I like the idea of things that nest or fit together, with each thing having its own particular place.

Forming the Bases

To create the bottom of each bowl in a nesting set, I start with circular templates cut from tarpaper. This material is durable and impervious to water, which makes it great to use over and over as a template for clay. Tarpaper can be found at home improvement stores, often in giant rolls, which are cumbersome, but will last forever. Using a compass, I trace four concentric circles, each about two inches smaller than the next in diameter. Cut four circles out of a

thin cotton bed sheet, each just slightly larger than the tarpaper circles. Since the bottoms are stacked during forming, so that each one conforms to the one below it, these fabric circles keep the stacked clay slabs from sticking together.

When rolling out slabs, rotate the slab so that it doesn't get stretched out in just one direction repeatedly, which can weaken the clay. I roll out my clay between ¼- to ⅛- inch thick, compressing it with a rib. I then use the template to trace the largest (bottom) circle of the nesting set and to move it into the plaster slump mold, smoothing it into the curve of the mold with a rubber rib (1).

Working from the largest to the smallest, place one of the fabric circles down, then lay the next slab circle on top. Use the rib to conform each slab to the one below it and repeat the process until all slabs are placed and rounded (2).

Building the Walls

After making the bases, roll out slabs for the walls of each piece of the set. Figure out the circumference for each bowl by wrapping a reinforced cloth tape measure (the kind you find in fabric stores) around each of the stacked bottoms, then roll out slabs, trying to conform roughly to those dimensions. In the case of my large nesting set, the wall of the largest bowl is 6 inches tall with a circumference of 52 inches. My second largest wall stands 5 inches tall, the third is 4 inches, while the smallest bowl has a height of 3 inches and measures 14 inches in circumference.

Once the walls have reached soft leather hard, taper the top edge or rim first with a stiff rubber rib then with an elephant ear sponge (3). Tapering the edges creates a visual lightness and sense of delicacy to the bowls.

After thinning out the rims, stand the slabs on edge to shape them into circles. The slabs should be stiff enough so they can stand this way without collapsing, yet soft enough that they are not in danger of cracking when curved. Keeping the slabs on the slightly softer side is also an enormous help when you're blending the seams together.

After forming a slab into a circle, flip it over, placing the tapered top end down, and score the bottom as well as the attachment area on the corresponding base, then apply slip to both scored areas. When attaching walls to each base, work from the inside smallest piece outward to the largest so your hands have space to move around (4). Use a fine-toothed flexible serrated rib to smooth the edges of the wall together. Join the two sides together at a 45° angle to enable the largest surface area point of contact (see 6). After the seam sets up slightly, add a thin coil to reinforce it (5), then smooth the seam repeatedly with a series of stiffer to softer rubber ribs. This helps both to smooth the seam as well as to compress it and prevent cracks while drying.

5. Add a thin coil, then compress and blend the seam together with a fine serrated rib and a soft rubber rib.

6. Work from the smallest to the largest bowl. Bevel, then attach the ends of the wall slabs.

7. Using bisque molds made from the hump mold, separate the pieces to allow for more even drying.

8. Add a wide, soft coil to reinforce and soften the seam then smooth with a rubber rib.

9. Turn the leather-hard bowl upside down and clean up the bottom using a medium soft rib.

10. Clean the outside seam where the base meets the wall with a Surform rasp, then smooth with a rib.

Continue to work from the inside out, attaching walls to each of the concentric circular bases. Since the largest bowl calls for a 52-inch long slab, which would be very challenging and awkward to work with, I piece together two or three shorter slabs to create the wall of the outermost pieces (6).

After all walls have been attached to all bases, allow the piece time to set up. The entire process start to finish takes several days.

Once the pieces have stiffened to leather hard, place the bowls into separate bisque molds (7) and add a fairly thick coil on the inside to reinforce the seam as well as to create a softer and smoother transition from the walls to the base of the piece (8). Smooth the coil into the seam, first with a serrated metal rib to remove some of the excess clay, then a slightly stiff rubber rib. I'm a huge fan of the Mudtools ribs. The yellow rib number Y2 has the perfect curve to create a nice transition in the bowl where the base meets the wall (see 9).

At this point, the bowls should be stiff enough to pick up and place upside down to work on cleaning up the bottom. Placing the upside down bowl on foam (to protect the rim) on a turntable, very gently smooth the bottom of the piece with a rib (9), filling in any indentations with very small coils of clay. Use a Surform rasp to clean up the outer edge where the wall meets the base (10). After using the rasp, go back and smooth this area over with a rib. The pressure from this clean-up work sometimes creates a bit of a bulge on the inside of the pot. It's important to keep flipping the piece over to a minimum, but if necessary, fix this bulge by adding coils or removing excess clay from the inside.

Once all pieces have been cleaned up on both the inside and outside, place them all back together, leaving them this way overnight under plastic to equalize in moisture. Allow to dry then bisque and glaze in the style of your choice.

EXPANDED FACETING

by Hank Murrow

Bowl, 4½ inches in diameter. The finished piece has a lively quality, which is a result of the dynamic process of opening the bowl after faceting.

Faceting a pot—slicing clay from the form using a fettling knife, wire tool, or sometimes a Surform tool—is usually done at the leatherhard stage. Several years ago I saw Joe Bennion facet bowls while they were still wet—just after the initial form was created—then continue to throw to create a stretched facet. Through experimentation, I created my own version of this process, as well as a wire tool with interchangeable wires to achieve different surface effects. Here's the method I use.

Process

To make a faceted bowl, begin with 2½ pounds of clay and open the form like a bowl, ribbing the bottom so you don't have to trim too much clay later (1). The bowl is kept to a cylindrical shape, keeping the wall thickness to about a ½ inch or a little more. I rib the inside as well to eliminate finger marks (2), and then give the rim a beveled profile with my chamois or rib (3).

The first cut with the wire tool trims away about a third of the wall and is cut parallel to the wall profile (4). Turn the wheel 180° and make the second cut, then 90° for the third cut and another 180° for the fourth. Cut the facets between the first four cuts (5) and smooth the edges with a wet finger.

Use a dull wooden rib and dry fingers to open the bowl, stretching the wire cuts and

dropping the rim (6). It takes about three passes to develop a full bowl shape. When the bowl has half-dried, turn it over and place on a sheet of foam rubber to protect the rim.

When ready to trim, place the bowl on a damp clay chuck and use a small piece of plastic as a bearing surface for the finger while trimming the outside (7). Follow by trimming the inside and finishing the foot with the chamois.

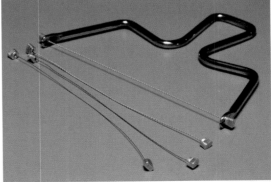

Hank developed this faceting tool (Hank's WireTool) with interchangeable wires, which yield different patterns in wet clay. (Note: Search "Hank's WireTool" on the internet for more information.)

BOWLS: FROM CIRCLE TO SQUARE

by Andrea Marquis

Ann Van Hoey transforms round shapes into a variety of forms inspired by origami and geometry, like those shown here from 2011. *Photo: Dries Van den Brande.*

The work of Belgian artist Ann Van Hoey consists of sculptural, handbuilt earthenware vessels along with a separate line of bone-china dinnerware that she designs for the European firm, Serax. Inspiration for her forms comes from *Étude Géométrique* (geometric study), which for Van Hoey is about "the marriage between the circle and the square." Origami is also an inspiration and Van Hoey's terracotta vessels are often darted in three sections to create a dynamic tension between the circle and the triangle.

Most of her forms are unglazed and the finished surface mimics the leather-hard stage when Van Hoey explains, "the clay is full of life." In her *Structure* series she investigates textured surfaces, she does this by texturing the molds that she uses to build her vessels. Despite her primary focus on unglazed surfaces, she has also experimented with color on some of her forms. These vessels have been professionally enameled at an auto body shop with car paint, producing a luscious surface that goes above and beyond glaze. The eye-catching forms tap into the psychology of our deepest desires through her choice of colors with serious caché, like Ferrari red and yellow.

While in the studio, Van Hoey engages in the making process with focus, precision, and intensity, but also with a sense of humor. She is very aware of the tension between her meditative clay process and the demands of the tech-savvy world outside the studio walls. There is evidence of this awareness and humor in her work, if you look closely on the side of the vessels in her *Social Clay* series, she has embossed the phrases, "Sent from my iPad," "sorry for the briefness," and "join me on Facebook."

The simplest forms are deceptively complex to make and for Van Hoey there are no short cuts or tricks. Her forming process has evolved over time through trial and error. Ideas for new pieces come naturally from the evolution of working in her studio, where patience and repetition are critical in achieving geometric perfection.

Hand Rolling Slabs

Van Hoey's forms begin as slabs and she uses commercial clay straight out of the bag. She prefers the clay to be soft and it's important that the clay be pliable but not sticky. After working with the Dutch artist Netty Janssens, she doesn't wedge her clay, preferring to align the clay particles by gradually thinning the slab as it's rolled out.

After every pass over the slab Van Hoey carefully pulls the clay up and off of the canvas to allow the slab to expand evenly and to allow the clay platelets to align, strengthening the slab. She then uses a soft red Mudtools rib to repeatedly smooth the slab throughout the rolling process. She carefully removes impurities and large grog particles as she makes her final passes over the slab. The clay slab must be perfect because most of her vessels are not glazed and the finished surfaces come from the fired bare clay.

Filling the Mold

To create her vessel forms, Van Hoey pieces rolled slabs into a half spherical plaster mold,

Tips for rolling slabs out by hand:

- Start with a slice of bagged clay that is pliable but not sticky.
- Use wooden slats of varying thicknesses (starting with two thicker slats and replacing them with progressively thinner slats as you work) to gauge and even out the thickness of the slab as it's rolled out.
- Begin rolling at the center of the slab, moving to the outer edges.
- Flip the slabs over after every roll to compress and align particles on both sides.
- Roll and thin the slabs gradually to keep the clay particles aligned.
- Once the slab has reached the approximate desired size and thickness, roll it one way, in the same direction.

usually 11–19 inches (30–50 cm) in diameter, that she purchased from a local clay supplier. In preparation for construction, she works with a paper pattern, developed through trial and error, to approximately fill her mold. She first lays the pattern on the slab (1) and then over the mold, eyeing the shape of the pattern to fit the mold's interior curve. Using a modified knife (see 5 inset), she cuts out a piece of clay that is approximately the same size and shape as the pattern (2). Next she uses a plastic circle with dividing lines as a guide to create marks on the top of her mold to help equally divide the vessel's circumference (3).

The mold and slab are cleaned and then inspected for contaminants and irregularities. As Van Hoey readies the piece, she flips and reverses the slab to ensure the perfect side faces outward and the finished surface has no imperfections. She carefully presses her cut slab into her mold; slowly expanding the slab into the curved shape (4). She notes that it's important this be done gradually and she takes great care to rib the clay up and down, and then back and forth with horizontal strokes so that it is evenly stretched and compressed.

Next, she trims the slab, cutting it on the top edge with her modified pen knife that allows the blade to be inserted at an angle (5). She locates the dividing marks on the mold that were created with the plastic circle template. Using each mark as a guide, she draws a line in the clay with her knife that only goes halfway through the slab—this prevents scratches on the interior of the mold. Then she removes the excess clay (6).

Van Hoey uses a total of three slabs to complete her form. When joining two slabs she compresses the edge of the slab, beveling it with

1. Lay the paper template over the smoothed out slab.

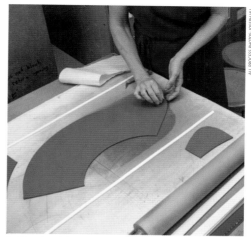

2. Cut the slab to the approximate shape and size of the template.

3. Use a circular dividing tool to mark the edge of the mold with guidelines for cutting the slab sections.

4. Press the cut slab into the mold, slowly expanding it to match the curve.

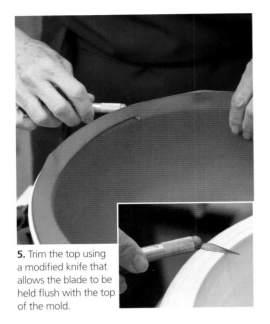

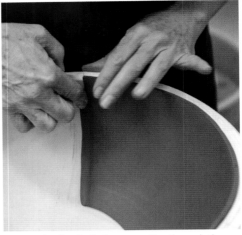

5. Trim the top using a modified knife that allows the blade to be held flush with the top of the mold.

6. Use a fettling knife to score a line through the excess clay along the vertical edge of the slab then remove it prior to adding the next slab to the plaster press mold.

7. Compress the slabs together gently before repeating the compression process with a rib.

8. Repeat the compression, refining, and smoothing process after adding the bottom slab.

her finger in order to create more surface area for the thin slab pieces to connect. She scores the edges, taking care not to scratch the mold. With light pressure she uses her finger to feel where the slabs overlap and cuts the top slab to fit. She removes the leftover piece with her pin tool and applies slip to the bottom slab.

Next, she gently compresses the slabs together with her finger (7). Using a semi-circular custom-made rib that she cut out of an old credit card, Van Hoey repeats the above step with more pressure. During this process she removes a little of the overlap of clay to make the wall thickness uniform. After the clay has been carefully ribbed, she removes the top edge with her modified knife.

She repeats this process, rolling out slabs, cutting out patterned pieces, joining them, then refining the form to make the vessel's sides.

9. Flip the mold upside down onto a bat and gently tap the bottom of the mold to release the form.

10. Smooth and compress the seams and to compress the entire outside of the vessel.

11. Cut darts into the form with scissors. The length and width of the darts guide the final shape.

She fills the bottom by approximating the shape and repeats the above steps, beveling the edges and scoring the clay form in the mold. Before attaching the bottom piece of clay to the form in the mold, Van Hoey stamps the bottom of the slab with her chop (potter's mark) and places the slab into the mold face down—this way impressing the stamp won't distort the final form. Compressing the slabs together she repeats

her refining and smoothing process (8). The refining process is very meditative. She notes that though it has been a slow evolution repeating the same technique, with practice she's been able to hone and continue to improve her forms.

Van Hoey smooths the bottom of the form, then moves the mold onto a pottery wheel for more clean up. She centers it by eye, then secures the mold to the wheel head with clay wad-

12. Gradually overlap the clay cuts, score and slip within the overlapped area and join.

13. Refine the seams using a wooden sculptor's thumb or rubber-tipped tool.

14. Scrape the rim with a metal rib to bevel it, then smooth and compress the edge.

Object, 10 in. (26 cm) in length, slab-built and press-molded earthenware, 2015. *Photo: Dries Van den Brande.*

ding and continues to compress the clay form against the mold and refine the thickness of its wall. She trims the top edge of the vessel one more time with her altered knife and then compresses it with her finger to finish the top edge.

Removing the Vessel Form

Timing is critical for Van Hoey's altering process. The clay must be at the perfect stage—firm enough to be handled out of the mold, but plas-

tic enough to fold without cracking. The vessel shape must be evenly pliable so it's important to avoid a draft that can lead to uneven drying. She lets her piece set up in the mold for 1–2 hours. She covers the mold with a bat and places it in a cardboard box. Closing the box reduces drafts and helps to equalize the moisture in and around the piece.

Van Hoey removes the piece from the mold by flipping it upside down on a bat and gently

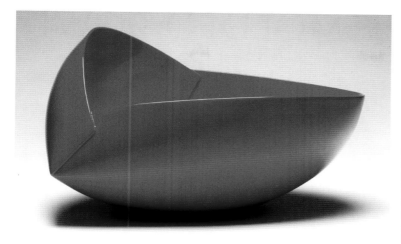

Object from the *Earthenware Ferrari* series, 16 in. (40 cm) in length, slab-built and press-molded earthenware, automotive paint, 2014. *Photo: Dries Van den Brande.*

tapping the mold to release the form (9). The upside-down form and bat go onto a banding wheel. Using the flat, wide side of a metal rib, she cleans the outside of seams where the slabs were joined together. She inspects the outside surface of the form for any irregularities—popping air bubbles and then using a red Mudtools rib to smooth the exterior surface (10).

Darting

Using her hands, Van Hoey flips the clay form right-side up and cradles it in a pillow. With her circular dividing tool (see 3), she establishes three equidistant points on the top edge of her form and makes a mark. Next, she measures how long she wants the dart to extend toward the bottom of the form as well as how wide she wants them to be, both of which will affect the final shape. These marks guide her as she cuts her darts.

With large, sharp, heavy-duty scissors, which create a cleaner, straighter cut, Van Hoey cuts through her form (11). She cuts next to the seams between the original slabs of clay used to make the form so that the seam will be underneath the dart and therefore concealed by it when the clay walls overlap. Next, she gradually folds and smooths the clay cuts to until they overlap. Then, with a needle tool, she marks the outline of the overlap. She scores and slips each side (12), making sure there's ample slip in the corners of the overlaps, which keeps the darts from pulling apart.

Finishing the Form

Van Hoey uses a wood sculptor's thumb to refine the seams (13), compressing them so there is absolutely no gap. The edges of the darts get dabbed with water and compressed. Small holes often appear at the bottom of the darts due to the movement of the folding process so she repairs them by touching them up with water and then using a wooden tool to compresses the area inside and out. She then smooths all of the seams' sides and joints with a red Mudtools rib and repeats this process until perfect. The clay form then gets covered in loose plastic and she smooths the rim the next day.

To finish the piece, Van Hoey scrapes the rim with a metal rib (14), beveling it slightly, and then refines the overlapping top edges with a wooden tool. She uses a damp sponge to smooth the exterior, removing finger marks on the outside edge—the inside doesn't get sponged. Finally, the bottom gets tapped slightly to flatten it out (this keeps it from rocking after firing) and the finished piece is slowly once fired to cone 1.

BLOCK MOLDED BOWL

by Tom Quest

I use wood forms and wood stamps to create my pottery designs. This dish uses an old wood moth stamp I made years ago for part of the surface design, and a wooden drape mold for the depth and shaping.

Tools to Make

After sketching a new idea, I work through test pieces of clay with a stamp before making templates, additional stamps, and a drape mold. For templates, I use plastic sheets used for quilt layouts found at fabric stores. I prefer this to tarpaper because I can see through it for registration. For this design, I created two templates—one for the outside shape and a second one for the pattern that creates a border and defines the interior areas (1).

While you can use many types of materials for drape molds, I normally choose wood. For this project I created a mold by cutting a 2×6 board to the shape I wanted then rounded the edges with a router (a Surform tool works well also). In designing a mold, be sure to consider the size of the object you want to make in order to determine the best size of your slab-to-form ratio for supporting the rim.

The type and age of clay is also important. I use a smooth, plastic clay body, which tears less when you stretch it over a form. New clay, which is generally less plastic, tears more than aged clay when stretched; older clay tends to be more plastic and forgiving. I do not use clay with grog because the impressions don't show up as nicely, and dragging grog across a surface can ruin the surface decoration.

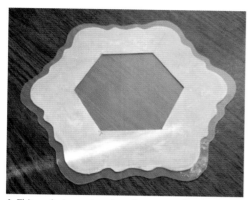

1. This project uses two templates—one for the form and one for defining sections for surface decorations.

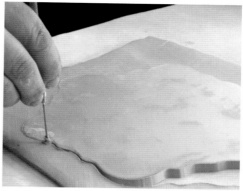

2. Roll out a ¼–5⁄16-inch-thick slab of clay, and cut out the form using the large template as a guide.

3. Place the smaller template on the slab and use a tool to press the edge of the template into the clay.

4. The small template also serves as a mask when adding background texture to the center of the slab.

Creating a Textured Slab Bowl

Roll out a ¼–5⁄16-inch-thick slab of clay. Smooth both sides with a soft rib to remove any canvas marks or surface flaws. When lifting and turning the slab, be careful to fully support it so you don't create a "bad memory" that causes it to warp in the firing. Lay the larger template on the slab and cut out the shape (2). Next, lay the second template with the cut-out hexagon on the slab and use a wood tool to push the plastic evenly into the clay around the perimeter (3). This defines the border and leaves a nice glaze transition line in the clay. Leave the template on the clay for the next step.

As part of my design I wanted a visual "gathering point" for the moths in the center of the bowl. While shopping in a costume shop, I found a nylon stocking with a spiderweb design. I stretched the stocking material over a wooden frame (4) then used a small roller to transfer the design. The template acts as a resist and only allows the impression in the hexagonal center (5). Round over the edges with a damp sponge, then carefully remove the template.

I created the moth stamp with a scroll saw and added details with a woodburning tool. The advantage of using wood stamps is that you can cut, carve, drill, sand, file, and wood burn what you need for your design while the clay is still wet. Spraying wood stamps with cooking oil or dusting them with cornstarch keeps them from sticking to the clay (6).

5. Define border and central areas, texture the background, then gently remove the smaller template.

6. Lightly spray wooden stamps with cooking spray so they won't stick to the clay.

7. By planning ahead and creating accurate templates, the stamped pattern fits the overall design.

8. Carefully place a drape mold in the center of the slab. Place a board or bat on top and flip the slab over.

Firmly press the stamp into the clay, repeating the pattern all around the form (7). Note how the "unstamped" portion of the clay between the moth and the spider web creates an interesting design with contrasting positive and negative space. Add additional details to complete the texturing.

Center the mold on the textured slab (8). For larger pieces, spray the mold with cooking spray or even lay a piece of newspaper cut to the same size as the mold to serve as a separator.

Carefully lay a second work board on top of the hexagonal block and lift the work up using the original large working board under the slab. Quickly flip the sandwiched block and slab over without altering the registration between the

clay and the wood. Carefully remove the original board (which is now on top) and the newspaper. The newspaper sticks to the clay so peel it back slowly so the registration of the hexagon block and the clay won't shift. At this point the clay begins to slump over the mold.

When you look carefully at the clay you'll notice how the stamped image has translated through the clay and is now visible on the bottom, in some designs this is helpful as to the location of pressure you use when forming. You'll also notice some wrinkles made by the newspaper, but these will be worked out later.

At this point it's very important not to rush! Moisten your fingers, then slowly apply gentle pressure on each corner of the piece (9). Use a

9. With moistened hands, slowly work the slab over the form as you rotate the piece on a banding wheel.

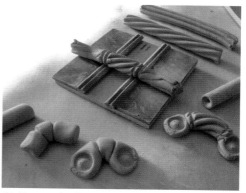

10. Feet can be formed using different strap handle techniques. The possibilities are endless.

banding wheel and rotate the piece to evenly apply a small amount of pressure to each corner. Move in very small, even steps otherwise the piece will warp when fired. Notice the position of the thumbs in relation to the outside shape and the hexagonal mold, which is clearly visible even though it is under the clay. Move your thumbs evenly up and down at each corner and continue to dip them in water to reduce drag. It's important to know when to stop; you want a slope to the sides of the bowl but don't overwork the clay until it cracks. As you do more projects with this technique, you'll discover how much you can feel through the clay where the impressions have been made.

Finishing Touches

To create the feet, there are many methods you can use. You can make a decorative coil foot by starting with a coil then rolling over it with a square stick at two opposing angles to segment it, then flatten the ends and press with a stamp (10).

I've created a collection of dowels with drilled countersinks in the ends. These are perfect tools for creating decorative touches as well as securely fastening feet or handles to your work. Another type of foot begins with an extruded ribbed coil. When twisted, it has a "barber pole" pattern. When you take this coil and roll it on a

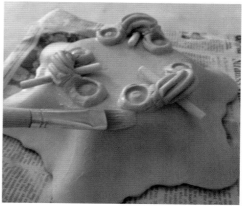

11. Strap feet serve a dual role in they can be used as lugs for picture hanging wire.

raised board that has parallel ridges as shown, it forms a decent end ring to visually finish the foot. Attach the decorative coiled feet to the bottom of the form using dowels to maintain an opening (11). Strap feet allow a user to display a form as a decorative hanging object. Lay a small light board on top to flatten the bottom surface that will contact the table then remove the dowels. Cover the piece to allow the moisture to even out.

Most of the trimming on the rim is done at the leather-hard stage to give it a nice rounded edge, and the entire surface is checked for cleanup. I usually allow the piece to dry for 10 to 14 days before bisque firing.

HUMP MOLDED OVAL BOWL

by Elisa Helland-Hansen

For nearly forty years I have been dedicated to making functional pots for use in everyday life—for preparing and storing food, for social events, and for meals.

I seek simplicity in form and a quiet expression. Subtle traces from the process are visible in my finished work like finger marks on handles or seams from joining parts. My work has reached its goal when it is filled with food.

My interest in utility is closely related to my love of cooking and making food. It feels so fundamental; every human being has to eat from something every day. Among my favorite items to make are ovenproof oval bowls of many designs. I find the oval shape is beautiful for serving most any dish.

Benefits of Design

There are several aspects I like about the design of this bowl: first the pattern created by the coils wrapped around the form, and second the strength the coils provide to the exterior both physically and aesthetically. I

1. Plaster hump mold with angled finger holes to pull the mold up and out of the clay form.

2. Cut the slab approximately ½-inch larger than the cardboard template. Bevel the V-shaped ends at a 45° angle.

3. Score and slip the bevels, place the slab onto the mold, then shape it to the form.

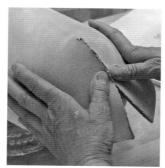

4. Press the seams of the slabs together so they conform to the shape of the mold.

5. Smooth the join and compress the clay, pushing it against the mold with a rib.

enjoy when the light sifts through the ribs at the bottom of the bowl, visually lifting the form slightly from the table. I also like when I'm serving food and the shape of a rounded spoon matches the curve of the bowl.

Hump Mold

My first oval bowl of this kind was made about 15 years ago. The original plaster hump mold has been broken and glued back together, but's still in use.

I used a plastic drainage tube to make my hump mold, which is 19 inches long, 6½ inches wide, and 4 inches high (1). My hump mold is solid and quite heavy, but I added four angled holes, made from clay coils, to the wet plaster

before it stiffened to make grips for pulling up the hump mold from the clay form.

Fitting a Template

To make a well-fitting template for the mold, start with a dry mold. Drape a thin sheet of clay over it, then cut and dart the slab to conform to the shape of the mold. When the clay has stiffened up a bit, cut a line through the clay at both ends of the mold up to where the shape flattens out. Have someone help you lift the slab off the mold and let it unfold to a flat slab on top of cardboard or a similar durable material. Draw a line around the slab and cut out the shape. This will be the template for making the actual oval bowl.

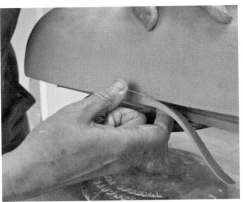

6. Use a wire tool to cut off any excess clay along the edge to make the rim level, then smooth the edge.

7. Extrude long, even coils and split each coil precisely in two halves with a knife.

Making the Bowl

Roll out a ¼-inch-thick slab. I use a heavily grogged (40%) fireclay, which is suitable for ovenware. You can use a finely grogged clay, which will reduce shrinkage and counteract warping, if you prefer a smooth surface. If your mold is smaller, the slab can be thinner. Place the template on the slab and cut ½ inch outside the cardboard along the parallel sides to ensure the clay will cover the mold completely (2). Be sure to cut the two V-shaped short ends at 45° angles so they can be attached later.

Let the slab dry to soft leather hard. It takes a little practice to learn the exact timing of moving the slab onto the hump mold. It needs to be stiff enough to lift up at the end without breaking, but still soft enough to be workable without cracking when stretch over the mold. I find it helpful to place a board that's slightly smaller than the mold onto a banding wheel and place the hump mold on top. This way I can rotate the form and access the rim.

Score the beveled V-shaped end cuts of the slab and add slip. Lift the slab at one end, then fold it over the mold with the bottom side toward the mold. Adjust the slab so that it lies symmetrically over the mold (3), then press the slab down in several movements until the clay is tightly draped around the mold. Press the scored parts together against the mold (4). Use a flexible metal rib to compress and scrape off excess clay to make the seam smooth (5).

Next, cut the rim of the bowl with a wire tool to create a level edge (6). Moisten the surface and use a soft rib to smooth the exterior. Let the bowl set up on the plaster mold for several hours.

Coil Decoration

Using softer clay (of the same clay body), extrude round coils that are approximately four-feet long. The thickness of the coil should not exceed twice the thickness of your bowl's rim. Slice each coil in half without distorting the shape (7). Measure the curve of your bowl and cut the coils slightly longer than that measurement.

Brush thick slip onto the middle part of the bowl, then wrap one sliced coil over the slipped area and press it firmly onto the shape without distorting the coil (8). Continue to add new slip and coils at regular intervals until the bowl is covered (9).

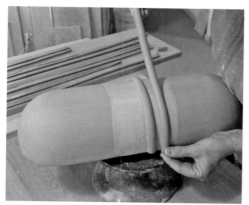

8. Brush thick slip onto the form in sections and press the coils onto the bowl.

9. Press each coil firmly to the bowl and ensure good attachment on every single one.

10. Using two flat boards, knock them several times horizontally to flatten the coils on the bottom.

11. The flattened coils on the bottom of the pot stabilize the form and allow it to sit flat.

Once all the coils are attached, check each one to ensure a secure attachment, especially at the curves, so they won't pop off during drying or firing. Brush a slip over the whole piece and let it dry to a soft leather hard—stiff enough to be removed from the mold without distorting the shape, but before cracks appear due to shrinkage.

Leveling the Bottom

Take the mold off of the banding wheel, set it onto a flat surface, place a flat board over the bottom coils, and knock it several times with another long board to flatten the coils on the bottom (10 and 11).

Gently turn the mold over, loosen the edges from the mold and pull the mold up by using the finger holes (12). Sometimes a crack forms at the curves. These can be easily mended, as long as the clay is still workable, by dripping slip in the crack and compressing it firmly. Use clay and a rounded rib to seal up the inside seam of the bowl.

Trimming the Rim

Measure the lowest height of your bowl and make a marking guide by drilling a hole into a square stick at the low height measurement and sliding a needle tool through the hole. Place the

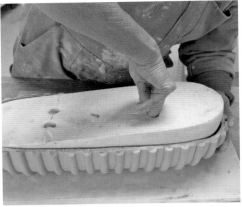

12. Loosen the edge of the rim slightly from the plaster to enable the mold to be lifted up and separated from the clay form.

13. Make a horizontal line around the bowl with a needle tool fitted into a square board. Cut off the rim with a sharp knife.

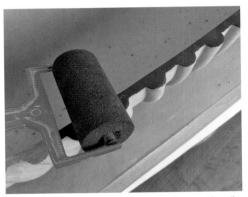

14. Smooth the edge of the rim several times with a rib and plastic sheet, then roll a colored slip onto the rim.

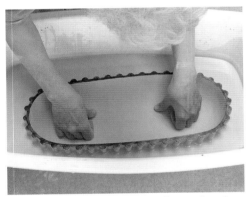

15. Press the bowl down horizontally into the tub until the glaze reaches the rim.

bowl on a flat, level board that's slightly wider and longer than the bowl. Place the board on a banding wheel and mark a horizontal line at this height with the needle tool around the whole bowl keeping the stick vertical while spinning the bowl (13).

Use a sharp knife to cut the edge of the bowl horizontally along the marked line. This will level the rim. Scrape the rim, then use a soft rib to smooth it, being careful to avoid distorting the coil pattern. To finish the rim, I use a strip of plastic to soften the edges.

To create a colored rim, apply a contrasting slip with a sponge roller (14). Now you can let the bowl dry. Place something flat on top of the bowl while it's drying to prevent warping, then bisque fire the bowl.

Glazing and Firing

I start the glazing process by using wax resist on areas where I don´t want any glaze. That can be both the flat rim and the bottom of the bowl. Without the wax resist, I find it difficult to clean off the glaze on the bottom because of the coils.

Oval bowl, slump molded with slabs, added coils, fired to cone 10 in a reduction atmosphere.

Next, glaze the interior with a food-safe liner glaze. Wipe off any excess glaze on the exterior or the rim. Let the liner dry completely before glazing the exterior.

Pour an exterior glaze into a large, plastic tub. Press the bowl down horizontally into the tub until the glaze reaches the rim (15). Lift the bowl up by pushing your fingers against the interior walls. Spraying is an alternative method for exterior glazing of this type of pot. If you spray the glaze, you won't need to make or have such a large volume of glaze.

The exterior glaze I use on most of my pots is a dry slip glaze that was introduced to me by English potter John Maltby in 1977 while I was still a student. It's applied on bisque ware and creates the best colors over a white slip containing alumina.

I glaze fire my oval bowls to cone 9 in a reduction atmosphere, but the 1-2-3 Maltby Slip Glaze works in neutral and oxidation atmospheres as well. The glaze is very sensitive to both thickness and atmosphere and produces a variety of hues according to the application and firing method.

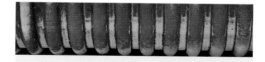

1-2-3 MALTBY SLIP GLAZE
Cone 9 Reduction

Custer Feldspar	1 part
Whiting	2 parts
China Clay (Kaolin)	3 parts

Add small percentages of different coloring oxides to produce color. Apply over a white slip containing alumina to achieve the best color results.

CLOVER DISH WITH SLUMPED BOTTOM

by Joe Singewald

The design for the clover dish began when I decided to study ceramics with Randy Johnston at the University of Wisconsin-River Falls. Randy taught me how to handbuild with soft slabs and how the tensile strength of clay can create beautiful, gentle curves. Many twists and turns later, the first clover dish was conceived out of desperation. I was a graduate student at Utah State when asked to teach an intermediate handbuilding class. Although coil- and slab-built pottery made up a percentage of my body of work, I wasn't confident in my slab-construc-

tion forms. At the time, I asked myself, "How can I excite students about slab building if I am not thrilled with it myself?" This challenged me to develop new ideas, which resulted in the clover dish.

Making a Paper Template

My clover dishes are constructed with a slump-mold technique. Making the form requires basic woodworking tools and skills. The desired shape is first cut from a paper template to scale. It's important to know how much your clay

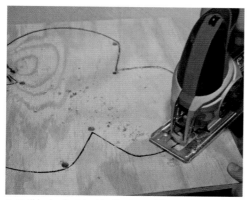

1. Drill holes just inside the traced form, then use the jigsaw to cut a precise slump mold.

2. To make a slab, stretch a wire between two notched sticks.

3. Pull the wire through a block of clay to make ½-inch thick slabs.

4. Each slab thickness is determined by the space between the end of the stick and the notches.

shrinkage is so that you can compensate for it in the template. You can use any shape, symmetrical or asymmetrical, large as a serving platter or as small as a soap dish.

Cutting a Wood Slump Mold

With a marker, transfer the paper pattern onto a piece of ¾-inch thick plywood that is at least one inch larger than the paper pattern in all dimensions. Use a drill and jigsaw to cut out the pattern (1). Start by drilling a hole just inside the traced form with a drill bit that is wider than the a jigsaw blade. Sometimes several holes make cutting complex forms easier. In this case, I cut three holes at each of the inner clover points. Next, slide the saw blade inside

a drilled hole and slowly begin cutting along the pattern. Once the form has been cut and removed, hand sand the inside edge. Softening and slightly rounding this edge helps prevent unwanted shearing of the clay. Now your slump form is ready to use.

Preparing a Slab

Roll a slab out to at least 1½ inches larger than the cut hole in all directions. The clay will stretch and thin as it slumps into the form so make the slab ½ inch thick. To reach the desired thickness, either use a rolling pin and wooden thickness guides or cut the slab using a "pocket slab roller" (2–4) a handy tool I made after seeing Randy Johnston's. To make a pocket slab roller, tape

5. Compress each side of the slab with a firm rib and then texture one side.

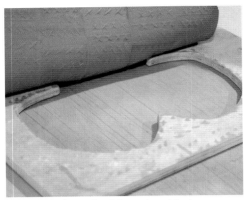

6. Carefully drape the slab, texture side down, over the plywood slump mold.

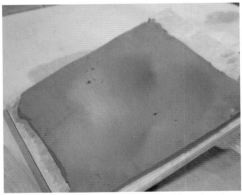

7. Tap all four of the edges of the mold against the tabletop to slump the clay.

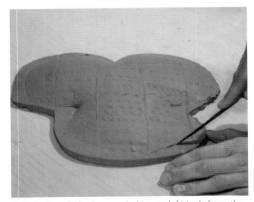

8. Cut a beveled edge, angled inward, ⅛ inch from the outside edge along the line made by the mold edge.

two scrap pieces of wood together, measure and mark them, then cut notches at regular intervals with a band saw. My sticks have different spacing on opposite sides, allowing different slab thicknesses depending on the project.

Next, compress each side of the slab with a firm rib and then texture one side. I make bisque clay rolling stamps, or cords for texture (5). The great thing about handbuilding with soft clay is how easy it is to impress while flat.

Slumping a Slab

Once textured, the clay is ready to be put in place. Drape the slab, texture side down, over the slump mold (6). Lifting the clay-covered

form from the tabletop immediately allows the clay to take shape. Tilting the form and tapping all four of the edges on a tabletop promotes further slumping (7).

Now set the board and slab on wooden blocks or kiln posts that are tall enough so the draped clay doesn't touch the table surface and allow the clay to become leather hard. I typically cover the slab with plastic and return the following day. The wooden form will absorb some of the clay's moisture overnight. Once leather hard, remove the slumped slab from the mold and gently flip it onto a table. Next, bevel the edge ⅛ inch from the outside edge. You will see a distinct line created from the wooden

9. Return the cut-out slab to a foam-lined slump form. The foam prevents the slab from slipping through.

10. Flatten clay coils and cut them in equal widths, then attach after slipping and scoring both parts.

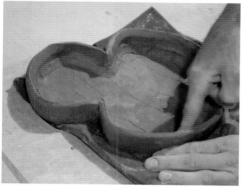

11. Add a coil to fill in the inner seam where the walls connect to the base and to each other.

12. Use a Surform to true up the sides and to create texture. Then pinch and refine the lip.

form (8). After placing foam on the mold (I reuse cone pack foam) return the clay to the form (9). The foam prevents the clay from falling through after being cut.

Adding Walls

To add the walls, start by flattening coils of clay and cut them into equal widths. An extruder works great if you have access to one. I make extruder dies from Masonite by cutting the wall cross section with a jigsaw in the same manner the clover mold was made. A string can be used to determine how long each of the three clover sides need to be. Next, attach the walls to the base slab after scoring and slipping both parts (10).

Cover the dish overnight, allowing the walls to become leather hard. Once this has occurred, add a worm-sized soft coil to fill in the inner seam where the walls connect to the base and where they connect to each other (11). I often texture the exterior walls with a paddle or rolling stamp. In this case, I used a Surform to true up the sides and create texture (12). At the same time, I pinch and refine the lip.

Adding Feet

The final step is adding three feet. Flipping the dish over onto foam protects the lip while feet are added. Roll out three angled coils, score

13. Score, apply slip, and attach three angled coils for feet. Once they're leather hard, cut and define their shape.

The side of the finished form showing the profile view and a detail of the rasped surface texture and shape of the cut feet.

The finished wood-fired clover dish showing the top profile.

one end of each, then score three spots on the bottom of the dish. Apply slip, then attach the coils. Be careful not to attach the feet too close to the center, as the form will become unstable and could tip during use. While the feet are still soft, flip the dish over and set it on a banding wheel. Turning the wheel, make sure the dish's lip is level and adjust as needed. Return the clover dish upside down to the foam and wait for the feet to become leather hard (again, I cover the piece and return the following day.) Once the feet are leather hard, cut and define their shape (13).

Making these forms requires several days and patience. It takes time for parts to become leather hard and it's best not to rush. I work on them in a series of three, making slight alterations to vary each one from the other.

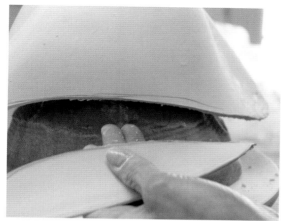

8. After these alterations, allow the bowl to rest and moisture content to even out, then cut the rim to the desired shape while supporting the bowl on foam chucks.

9. Smooth and refine all surfaces with a damp sponge. Pay careful attention to softening the cut edge of the rim.

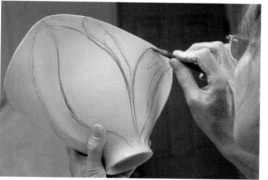

10. Once the form is compelte, start the proecess of carving the surface. Using a charcoal pencil, mark the surface for carving the design.

11. Carve the surface, following the drawn lines. Tools should range from blunt tools for softer clay to very sharp-edged tools for bone dry clay.

may have to rest the bowl at many stages of this process if it gets too wet. Put it back in the sealed container and work on another piece until it is evenly moist again.

I start by marking areas where I want to split and alter the wall with a charcoal pencil, then score these lines lightly (1). Next, I attach a slab or coil over the scored line, with the narrow end at the base. I pinch the attachment until it stands out like a fin from the main body (2). I repeat the process on the other side, but only work on fur-

ther altering one side at a time (3). After attaching the fins, I dunk the piece in throwing water that has a few drops of vinegar added to deflocculate the mixture (4). The movement is a fast dunk that allows the porcelain to instantly soak water back into its walls. I only dunk one side at a time, even if I want to alter both sides. When working this way, be sure to dry off any excess water puddles to prevent weak spots.

Using a sharp cutting tool, I slice through the wall of the pot along the curve next to the

12. *An Ocean Wide (Ocean series)*, 7 in. (18 cm) in height, wheel-thrown and altered bowl with glazed interior and polished exterior.

attached flange (5). Carefully pull one side of the wall away, score the cut edge of the wall and the end of the flange and attach the two (6). After securing the seams, I pinch them to an even thickness with the rest of the wall (7), and shape both sides until they are blended and the curve is consistent. After altering the sides, I place the piece upside down on a foam chuck, and cut the rim to the desired shape (8). Once the curves are cut, I refine them and smooth all of the surfaces with a damp sponge (9). With the form complete, I am ready to move on to carving the surface, and mark out the design using a charcoal pencil (10). Next, I carve the design using a variety of tools (11). My carving tools range from blunt for softer clay to very sharp edges for bone dry clay. You must still control the humidity of the clay to reduce the risks of cracking. Cracks in soft clay can be fixed without trouble, but repaired cracks in dry clay will appear as a scar in the translucency of the final object.

Primary qualities of porcelain are translucency and whiteness.

13. Antoinette Badenhorst working at the potters' wheel in her studio.

SPLASH BOWLS

by Aysha Peltz

I adopted the term splash bowl years ago to refer to a family of forms that interest me. The name comes from their resemblance to the iconic photograph, *Milk Drop Coronet*, by Doc Edgerton (http://edgerton-digital-collections.org). The similarity of form is rather obvious, but more important to me was the elegance with which the image arrests a moment in time. In this regard, the exposure of film to light is not unlike the exposure of clay to fire.

Touch and Utility

It was early in undergraduate school when I first started to throw with porcelain. I was seduced by porcelain's whiteness and its responsiveness to my touch. These qualities made it impossible for me not to manipulate the clay just after it was thrown. Arguably, it was too early for me to be using this challenging material (porcelain) but as a result I came up with ways of working that allowed me to achieve interesting forms not through consummate throwing but by the cutting, folding, ripping, and stacking of my thrown pots. Years went by and my throwing skills improved but this love of wet manipulation remained integral to my work.

The forms I make reference utility, the familiarity of these forms creating an invitation to look further. The thrown pots themselves are built on basic geometries, cylinders or cones

Pink Platter, 21 in. (53 cm) in diameter, white stoneware, oxidation fired to cone 10, 2004.

Splash Bowl, 15 in. (38 cm) in diameter, porcelain, fired in oxidation to cone 10, 2014.

nal state. Low, open forms are a challenge because as viewers we have access to both inside and out. With these kinds of forms, the act of pushing on the side wall is often too evident in the finished piece, the obviousness of the process complicating the viewer's ability to find other references.

Developing and Refining the Form

About the time I was struggling with how to build these forms two things happened. The first was seeing a landscape very different than that of New England where I had lived much of my life. On a trip to Idaho, I was struck by the sense of space implied by mountains bordering vast open valleys. The suggestion of the bowl/platter forms I had been working on was clear. Then, following that trip, I saw Peter Voulkos make a series of platters during a workshop at Alfred University. Watching the physicality and sensitivity that went into making those huge pots energized and clarified for me what excited me about making. Working on a body-sized scale while throwing a pot allowed for big physical gestures and small intimate moments with the material. Seeing that happen so confidently for Voulkos charged and challenged me to explore scale and gesture in my own work more freely.

Larger-scale pots can obscure their association with use and help the viewer to access the other references that the pots carry. Most of these splash bowls range between 20–50 pounds, the larger ones are more platters than bowls. Without knowing it at the time, Idaho and Voulkos had crept into my work and I became interested in working in relationship to my body size, throwing vases that were as tall as my arm was long and platters as big as I could physically manage. I started to see form more

varying in proportion or perhaps a suggestion of volume. To these forms I add layers of texture and dimensional line that respond to and emphasize the actions to follow. The alteration is a push into the inside or outside of the wall, expanding the texture from behind, creating curves and swells in the form. This way of working naturally creates suggestions of terrain, body, and flora; parched earth, a body in motion, or the imminent decay of something overripe. I fire the pots under fluid, translucent glazes preserving these moments in fired clay.

I want my pots to feel as though they have grown naturally and comfortably into their fi-

1. Add a 12-pound ball of clay to a low, wide, smooth, centered mound.

2. Throw a low, wide cylinder.

3. Create a double rim by pushing a knife through a sponge.

4. Create surface texture using a modified cut credit card.

5. Add definition with another cut credit card at the base of the cylinder.

6. Using a thick throwing sponge, begin to push in and up from the outside of the cylinder.

clearly as the curves and shapes became proportionate to me.

Process

Most recently, my focus has been on a somewhat smaller *Splash Bowl* form. Teaching, motherhood, and an awareness of the limits of my strength and energy have made making these *Splash Bowls* more practical than platters. Even at this smaller scale I protect my body by only wedging 12 pounds of soft clay at a time. I center 12 pounds, then I sequentially add

7, 8. Repeat these pushes symmetrically around the outside of the pot.

9, 10. Use calipers to mark depth and spacing on the exterior sidewall and rim.

12-pound balls atop one another until I work up to the weight needed (1). Each time a ball is added I make sure the centered clay is low, wide, smooth, and dry so that it can accept the convex form of the next 12 pounds. As I add balls of clay, I push the centered mass lower and wider until all the clay is added and its shape is close to the width of the intended pot.

Depending on what form I am making, I throw a simple structure on the wheel, in this case a low, wide cylinder. The walls are fairly thick, about ⅜ inch, so my alterations can be more forceful without pushing through the wall of the pot (2). At this stage, I give careful consideration to how I form the rim (3). Though much of the rim will be cut away, thoughtful articulation and perhaps a double or split rim will provide a nice detail in the sections that remain after I have cut parts away.

I want to have different qualities of line throughout these pots. The surface textures created from a cut credit card highlights the moment of pushing; lines expand and at times crack and begin to reference earth and terrain (4). Thicker thrown ledges and scalloped-foot profiles become more prominent and create areas where glaze can begin to pool and spill (5).

Once texture and line are added to the interior I can begin to push the pot. At this stage I stop the wheel and advance it by hand. I turn the piece so that it can be pushed, squared, cut, folded or ripped. The pot must remain attached to the bat to resist being moved by the force of my alterations. The inside wall is first dusted with cornstarch so that my hand does not stick to the surface (6). Using a thick throwing sponge I begin to push in and up from the outside of the cylinder, the sponge obscures the

11. Cut out half-circles, based on the caliper measurements that were taken.

12. Fold out then score and slip the remaining sections of rim to close the flaps.

13. The folding of the rim begins to connect the inside and outside of the pot.

14. Smooth the bottom surface with a soft rib and refine the edges.

evidence of my hand (7 and 8). I use my inside hand to support the interior wall.

This is the most satisfying moment in the process of making these pots. How the surface responds to this push is always surprising and often beautiful. I do not know exactly what the finished piece will look like. Variations occur based on wall thickness, wetness of the clay, and the texture and lines I have built into the form and the focus of my hand's pressure.

I address the rim through a process of cutting and folding. I use calipers to mark depth and spacing on the exterior side-wall and rim (9 and 10). Then, I cut out repeated shapes at regular spaces around its circumference (11). The remaining sections of rim are folded out and onto themselves again stretching the inside texture (12 and 13). By pulling the inte-

rior over the exterior wall, this folding of the rim begins to connect the inside and outside of the pot.

To finish these pots, I wait until they are leather hard and can be flipped onto a foam-covered chuck. I do not trim a recessed foot-ring, but smooth the bottom surface with a soft rib (14). The outer exterior edge is defined with a rib and cleaned up with a sponge.

Most good pots, whether functional or not, conjure associations beyond use. My pleasure in making these pieces is being lost in their landscape, imagining myself in a terrain. Connected to my delight in this journey is the phenomenon that occurs when I push against a thrown, textured form to reveal something of the properties of clay. It is for these reasons that I am compelled to continue working this way.